THE FORGOTTEN STANDARDS

FOR WOMEN

THE FORGOTTEN STANDARDS

FOR WOMEN

Standards the World Forgot —
and the Women Who Carry Them Anyway

GEOFFREY ARBUCKLE

CANE Enterprises Publishing, LLC

THE FORGOTTEN STANDARDS FOR WOMEN

Standards the World Forgot — and the Women Who Carry Them Anyway

Published by CANE Enterprises Publishing, LLC
Kansas City, Missouri

Scripture quotations are taken from public-domain translations unless otherwise noted. Attributions to contemporary authors and public figures are the author's best understanding at the time of writing; where attribution is uncertain, the phrase "attributed to" is used.

The content of this book reflects the author's convictions and is offered for reflection, not as a substitute for pastoral counsel, medical advice, mental-health care, or legal guidance. Readers are encouraged to seek qualified professionals for matters requiring such expertise.

ISBN 979-8-9957319-6-2 (eBook)
ISBN 979-8-9957319-7-9 (Paperback)
ISBN 979-8-9957319-8-6 (Hardcover)

First Edition
Printed in the United States of America

DEDICATION

To my mother, Mary Arbuckle —

who taught me what a mother is by being one. Through example, through sacrifice, through hours given that no one ever counted, through the quiet, daily refusal to give less than her whole self — she shaped a home, she shaped her children, and she shaped me. The love she gave was never performed. It was lived. Every standard in this book that has anything to do with motherhood, I learned at her feet first.

To my wife, China Polly Arbuckle —

a Proverbs 31 woman in the flesh. Her godliness is not a posture; it is the architecture of her life. She has loved unyieldingly when it cost her, persevered when there was nothing left to draw from, and endured seasons that would have broken a lesser woman. Her grace, her mercy, and her forgiveness have rebuilt me more times than I can name. The standards in this book are her standards. I am married to the proof of them.

To my daughter, Madison Nicole —

who carries the same fire her mother carries. Her godliness, her endurance, her capacity for love and forgiveness, are already shaping the woman she is becoming. This book exists, in part, so that what was almost lost would be remembered for her — and for the daughters she may one day raise. Every page is, in some measure, a letter to her.

———

And to three women whose fingerprints are on the man who wrote this book —

my grandmother Annis, who showed me that strength and tenderness are the same trait wearing two coats; my grandmother Arbuckle, whose steady, ordinary faithfulness is the kind history rarely records and families never forget; and my aunt Maurine, whose love arrived at exactly the moments it was most needed and never once asked to be counted. The forgotten standards in this book were not forgotten by them. They simply lived them.

— G.A.

CONTENTS

PREFACE

I am not a woman.

I want to address that directly, on the first page, before we go any further. This book was written by a man. And the first reasonable question any woman might ask is: what business does a man have writing a book for women?

Here is my answer.

I have a wife who taught me what a woman is capable of when she decides to stop apologizing for the way God made her. I have a grown daughter I pour into every day — a young woman whose life is one of the reasons this book exists. I have friends, sisters-in-law, a mother, and the memory of grandmothers whose strength and softness built me long before I knew enough to thank them. And I have watched, for the better part of two decades, as the culture has systematically lied to the women I love about who they are, what they're worth, and what they were made for.

I am tired of watching it.

This is the third book in *The Forgotten Standards* series. The first was written for everyone. The second was written for men — a book I wrote because I watched a generation of boys grow up without anyone telling them what it meant to be a man, and I refused to let that silence continue. This book is the companion to that one. Not because women are a second thought, but because women deserve their own book — not an addendum, not a footnote, not a softer version of what was written for men. Something that speaks to the particular arena a woman walks in, with the same directness and the same fire.

I want to say clearly what this book is not.

It is not the version of biblical womanhood that strips women of their voice, their intellect, their agency, or their calling. I have no interest in that version. Neither did Jesus. He spoke to the Samaritan woman at the well when no rabbi would. He let Mary of Bethany sit at His feet as a student when the culture said women couldn't learn. He appeared first to women after His resurrection — at a time when their testimony was not even admissible in a court of law. He never diminished, sidelined, or patronized a single woman who encountered Him. That is the standard this book is built on.

It is also not a reactive, culture-war book that defines women only by what they are against. The world does not need more women who are angry. It needs more women who are anchored. That is a different thing entirely.

And it is not the Instagram-blessed, curated-perfection version of womanhood that has convinced millions of women they are failing at a life nobody is actually living. That version has done enough damage. I am not interested in adding to it.

What this book is: one hundred lists across ten categories, covering every major arena a woman walks in — her identity, her sisterhood, her motherhood, her marriage, her leadership, her work, her body, her mind, her legacy, her faith. Ten items per list. Each item direct. Each item rooted. Each item forged in observation of the women I love and the women I have watched walk in quiet strength while the world told them they were too much or not enough.

The standards in this book were not invented by me. They are old. Older than the culture. Older than the feminism that reacted against a brokenness the church had helped create. Older than the patriarchy that reduced women to roles instead of persons. These standards go back to the opening chapter of Genesis, where a woman was made in the image of God and given the same authority to fill, subdue, and steward as the man standing next to her.

They were not lost. They were abandoned. And it is time to pick them back up.

My qualifications for writing this book are limited. I want to acknowledge that openly. I have never carried a child. I have never nursed one. I have never walked into a room and been judged on the length of my skirt or the softness of my voice. I have not been told to smile more, talk less, or shrink to make someone else comfortable. I am writing from the outside of an experience I will never have.

But I have watched. And I have listened. And I have loved women who have lived these realities and come through the other side. This book is the fruit of their witness, filtered through my words, grounded in the Scripture we share, and directed at a culture that has forgotten what a woman is worth.

If you are a woman, I hope it gives language to something you have always known but could not quite say. If you are a young woman, I hope it hands you a map for a terrain nobody is willing to describe honestly anymore. If you are a woman who has been told, in subtle ways or direct ones, that you are too much or not enough, I hope this book becomes the rebuttal.

And if you are a man who picked this up because the woman in your life is in it, I hope it changes the way you see her.

The standards are not lost. They are waiting to be remembered.

Pick them back up.

— *Geoffrey Arbuckle*

Kansas City, Missouri

INTRODUCTION

The world has a problem with women.

Not because women are too emotional. Not because women are too ambitious. Not because women are too soft or too strong or too quiet or too loud. The world has a problem with women because women, when they are standing in the fullness of who God made them to be, refuse to be flattened into the shapes the culture is trying to press them into.

A woman in her fullness is not manageable. And the world prefers manageable.

So the world has spent the last century telling women what they must be to be acceptable. At first it told them they must be quiet — domestic, decorative, and deferential. When that lie collapsed, the world told them they must be loud — independent, hardened, and driven. When that lie exhausted them, the world told them they must be both — the career, the marriage, the children, the body, the friendships, the platform — all simultaneously, all flawlessly, all captured for public consumption.

Each version of the lie has done its damage. Each has produced a generation of women who woke up at some point, looked at their lives, and wondered how they had ended up so exhausted trying to become someone they were never supposed to be.

This book is a rebuttal.

It is not an argument against the progress women have made. It is an argument for a woman's right to step off the treadmill the culture has built — the one that measures her by metrics she did not choose, ranks her against women she has never met, and demands that she produce more, look better, feel less, and never rest. That treadmill is not liberation. It is a newer, glossier cage. And the women who have been running on it the longest are often the ones most desperate to get off.

The standards in this book are not new standards. They are old. They are the standards that describe the woman the book of Proverbs calls "a wife of noble character" — a woman whose worth is "far more than rubies," who "is clothed with strength and dignity," who "laughs at the days to come," who "speaks with wisdom," whose "children arise and call her blessed." That description, read honestly, is not a portrait of a submissive, quiet, domestic woman with no agency. It is a portrait of a working woman, a thinking woman, a wealthy woman, a generous woman, a strong woman — a woman whose life is wide and deep and full, and who fears God above all else.

That is the standard.

The world has replaced it with an endless scroll of women who are airbrushed, algorithmically curated, and quietly miserable. The women on the screens are not free. They are performing freedom for a camera. The difference matters.

This book is written for women who have looked at that performance and recognized it as theater — and who are ready to walk offstage and discover what a real life actually looks like.

Ten categories. Ten lists per category. Ten items per list. One hundred lists, one thousand items, covering every arena a woman walks in. Each item written to be read slowly, lived with, and returned to.

You will not agree with every standard. You are not supposed to. The goal of this book is not your agreement. The goal is to put language to things you have always sensed but have not been able to say out loud — because the culture made sure you would not have the vocabulary.

Here is the vocabulary.

Use it.

And remember this, before you turn the next page: the woman the culture is asking you to be is not the woman God made you. The shrinking, the performing, the apologizing, the comparison, the exhaustion — none of that came from Him. It was imposed on you. It can be put down.

Put it down.

Pick these up instead.

They were always yours.

CATEGORY ONE

Womanhood & Identity

List 1: Ten Marks of a Woman Who Knows Who She Is

She doesn't need the room's approval to walk into it. — A woman who knows who she is enters every space — the boardroom, the kitchen, the church, the crisis — with the quiet certainty that she belongs. Not because she earned the invitation. Because the God who made her placed her there on purpose. She doesn't scan the room for validation. She doesn't shrink to make others comfortable. She doesn't inflate to make herself feel significant. She simply is. And that kind of presence — unhurried, unforced, unshakeable — is the rarest thing in any room she enters.

She defines herself by what God says, not what the world measures. — The world measures a woman by her waist, her income, her followers, her marital status, her productivity, and the curated version of her life she projects onto a screen. God measures her by her heart. The woman who knows who she is has stopped letting the scoreboard define her and has started letting the Creator do it instead. She is fearfully and wonderfully made. She is chosen. She is loved. And no algorithm, no mirror, no comparison can override what the One who designed her has already declared.

She is strong without apologizing for it. — Somewhere along the way, the world told women that strength was unfeminine — that a strong woman was intimidating, aggressive, too much. That is a lie. The Proverbs 31 woman is clothed in strength and dignity, and she laughs without fear of the future. She didn't apologize for it. Neither should you. Strength in a woman is not a flaw to be managed. It is a gift to be wielded — for her family, her community, and every person fortunate enough to be under her influence.

She is gentle without confusing it with weakness. — Gentleness is not the absence of power. It is the control of it. The woman who can speak softly when she has every right to scream, who can extend grace when she has every reason to withhold it, who can hold a broken person without falling apart herself — that woman is not weak. She is operating at a level of emotional and spiritual strength that most people will never reach. Gentleness is strength under restraint. And it is devastatingly powerful.

She doesn't need to tear another woman down to stand up. — A woman who is secure in her identity has no need to diminish someone else's. She can celebrate another woman's beauty without questioning her own. She can applaud another woman's success without interpreting it as her failure. She can walk beside someone whose gifts are different from hers without feeling threatened. Comparison is the disease of the insecure. The woman who knows who she is has been cured of it — not by having more, but by knowing whose she is.

She owns her past without being owned by it. — The mistakes. The regret. The season she'd rather forget. The relationship that broke her. The failure she carries. A woman who knows who she is doesn't pretend those chapters don't exist. She doesn't hide them, and she doesn't worship them. She acknowledges them, learns from them, and walks forward — carrying the scar as evidence that she survived, not as a chain that keeps her tethered to what was.

She speaks with conviction and listens with humility. — She has opinions, and she holds them. She has a voice, and she uses it. But she also knows when to close her mouth and open her ears — because a woman of conviction without humility is a bulldozer, and a woman of humility without conviction is a doormat. Both fail. The woman who balances the two — who speaks when it matters and listens when it counts — is the woman whose words carry weight precisely because she doesn't waste them.

She guards her peace like it's sacred — because it is. — She has learned that not every argument needs her participation, not every opinion needs her response, and not every crisis needs her anxiety. She has drawn a line around her peace and she defends it — not with walls, but with boundaries. She says no without guilt. She steps back without apology. She protects her inner stillness because she knows that the woman who loses her peace loses her ability to function in every other role she carries.

She knows that her value is not a function of her usefulness. — The world will try to measure her by what she produces — the meals, the reports, the emotional labor, the clean house, the balanced schedule. And when she stops producing, the world will tell her she's less. That is a lie. Her value was established before she did a single thing — before the first report, the first diaper, the first dollar earned. She was loved before she was useful. And the woman who internalizes that truth will never again confuse her output with her worth.

She is becoming. — She is not finished. She is not behind. She is not the final version of herself. She is a woman in motion — growing, learning, failing, recovering, deepening. And the mark of a woman who knows who she is, paradoxically, is that she knows she is still becoming. She holds her current self with grace while reaching toward the woman God is shaping her to be. That tension — between who she is and who she's becoming — is not a failure. It is the evidence that she is alive.

List 2: Ten Lies the World Tells Women About Their Worth

"Your value depends on your appearance." — The world has built a multi-billion-dollar industry on making women feel inadequate about the way they look. Every advertisement, every filter, every retouched image whispers the same message: you are not enough as you are. It is the oldest lie in the playbook — and the most profitable. A woman who believes her value is tied to her appearance will spend her entire life chasing a standard that was designed to move. The woman who roots her value in the image of God — the One who designed her face, her frame, her features — has stepped off the treadmill permanently.

"Your worth is measured by your productivity." — The hustle culture doesn't discriminate. It tells women that they must produce, perform, and prove their value through output — a career, a clean house, a curated social presence, children who behave, a marriage that looks effortless. And when the woman slows down — when she rests, when she pauses, when she simply exists without accomplishing — the world tells her she's falling behind. But worth is not earned through motion. It is inherited through creation. You were worthy before you produced a single thing.

"You can have it all — and you should." — This is perhaps the cruelest lie the world tells modern women. It promises that a woman can be the perfect mother, the perfect wife, the perfect professional, the perfect friend, and the perfect version of herself — all simultaneously, all flawlessly. And when she inevitably cannot sustain that pace, the world doesn't blame the lie. It blames her. The truth is that no woman can have it all at the same time. She can have what matters — but only if she has the wisdom to choose it and the courage to release the rest.

"Independence is the highest virtue." — The culture has elevated independence to the status of religion — and in the process, it has convinced women that needing anyone is weakness. That depending on a husband is regression. That leaning on a friend is fragility. That relying on God is a crutch. This is a lie dressed as empowerment. The strongest women in history were not the ones who needed no one. They were the ones who knew who to lean on — and were humble enough to do it.

"You should be further along by now." — The timeline lie is devastating because it attacks silently. By twenty-five, you should be established. By thirty, you should be married. By thirty-five, you should have children. By forty, you should have figured it out. Says who? God's timeline has never matched the world's spreadsheet. Sarah had Isaac at ninety. Ruth found Boaz in the middle of poverty. Your life is not behind. It is unfolding at the pace of the One who writes it.

"Your voice doesn't matter." — In boardrooms. In churches. In families. In public. The message is sometimes spoken and sometimes just felt: sit down, be quiet, let someone else lead. This lie has silenced generations of women whose voices carried the exact wisdom the room needed. Your voice matters. Your perspective matters. Your experience matters. The God who gave you a mouth intended for you to use it — with wisdom, with conviction, and without apology.

"You are what others think of you." — The opinions of others have become a prison for modern women. Every comment, every look, every silence is analyzed for its verdict on her worth. She is living in a courtroom that never adjourns — with a jury that is never satisfied. The woman who escapes this lie is the woman who stops showing up for the trial. What others think of you is their business. What God says about you is the only verdict that holds.

"Strong women don't cry." — This lie tells women that emotional expression is a liability — that tears are a sign of fragility, that vulnerability is a weakness to be managed. It produces women who suppress their grief, swallow their pain, and perform strength while crumbling inside. The truth is the opposite. The strongest women are the ones who can weep without shame — because they are honest enough to feel and brave enough to show it. Tears are not weakness. They are the body's testimony that something mattered.

"Your best years are behind you." — This lie arrives with every birthday after thirty — and it accelerates with every decade. It tells women that youth was the gift and aging is the punishment. That relevance expires. That beauty fades. That purpose diminishes. It is a lie. Some of the most powerful, purposeful, impactful seasons of a woman's life happen after the world tells her she's past her prime. Ask Ruth. Ask Naomi. Ask the woman who finally found her voice at fifty-five.

"You are too much — or not enough." — The world will never get the dosage right. If you're passionate, you're too much. If you're quiet, you're not enough. If you're ambitious, you're aggressive. If you're content, you lack drive. The target moves every time you get close — because the target was never meant to be reached. The woman who stops trying to be the right amount and starts being the full version of who God made her is the woman who finally breathes.

List 3: Ten Ways to Define Yourself Before the Culture Does It for You

Start with Scripture, not with the screen. — Before you scroll, before the algorithm tells you who to be and what to want, open the Word. Let God set the tone for your identity before the world tries to. The woman who begins her day in scripture has an anchor the woman who begins her day on a screen does not. One is rooted. The other is reactive.

Name the voices you've been listening to — and evaluate them. — Who has been defining you? The mother who said you weren't pretty enough? The ex who said you'd never change? The culture that says you should look, act, earn, and live a certain way? Name the voice. Then ask: does this voice have the authority to define me? If the answer is no — and it almost always is — silence it. Replace it with the voice that does.

Write your own identity statement — and root it in truth. — "I am a woman who loves God, serves her family, uses her gifts with courage, and refuses to be defined by what the world values." That's a start. Write your own. Read it daily. Not as an affirmation exercise — as a declaration of war against every lie that has ever tried to shrink you. A woman who has defined herself on paper is harder to redefine by circumstance.

Stop curating and start living. — The version of you that exists on the screen is not you. It is an edited, filtered, captioned performance. And the more time you spend building the performance, the less time you spend living the life. A woman who defines herself before the culture does is a woman who lives in the real world — messy, unfiltered, uncaptioned — and finds her identity there, not in the applause of strangers.

Choose your inputs deliberately. — What you consume shapes who you become. The podcasts, the accounts you follow, the content that fills your quiet hours — all of it is forming you, whether you realize it or not. A woman who wants to define herself before the culture does must curate her inputs with the same seriousness she gives to her diet. Feed on truth. Starve the noise.

Develop convictions that don't bend with the trend. — The woman who stands on conviction is unmovable. The woman who stands on trends is a weathervane. Know what you believe about marriage. About motherhood. About faith. About purity. About how to treat people. And when the wind changes — and it will — stand anyway. Convictions are not popular. They are permanent. And permanent is the only foundation worth building a life on.

Practice saying no without explaining. — "No" is a complete sentence. It does not require a paragraph of justification, a list of excuses, or the approval of the person hearing it. The woman who can say no without guilt is the woman who has decided that her identity is not dependent on other people's comfort. That is freedom. Use it.

Invest in your mind. — Read books that challenge you. Study subjects that fascinate you. Pursue learning that has nothing to do with your job or your role. A woman who develops her intellect builds an identity that cannot be reduced to her appearance, her marital status, or her productivity. She is interesting because she is interested — and that depth becomes the foundation of a self that no cultural shift can shake.

Surround yourself with women who are becoming, not performing. — The women in your circle either reinforce the truth or amplify the lie. Find women who are honest about their failures, generous with their encouragement, and relentless in their pursuit of God. Those women will sharpen you. The ones who perform — who curate, who compete, who compare — will slowly erode the identity you're trying to build.

Let God finish the work. — You will not define yourself in a single afternoon. Identity is built over years — through trial, through failure, through faithfulness, through the slow work of becoming the woman God intended. Let Him work. Stop rushing the process. Stop demanding a finished product. The woman who lets God define her in His timing is the woman who arrives at an identity the world cannot replicate, cannot market, and cannot destroy.

List 4: Ten Things Every Woman Should Know Before She Turns Thirty

Your body is not the enemy. — It will change. It will expand and contract. It will carry scars, stretch marks, and the evidence of every season it's walked you through. The sooner you stop fighting it and start honoring it, the sooner you'll discover that your body was never the problem. The world's definition of it was.

Not every relationship deserves your loyalty. — Some people are in your life for a reason. Some are there for a season. And some should have left three seasons ago. A woman who knows the difference — and has the courage to enforce it — will spend her thirties with a circle that strengthens her rather than a crowd that drains her.

Loneliness is not a disease. — It is a season. And it is not solved by a relationship, a marriage, a child, or a following. It is solved by learning to sit with yourself — honestly, quietly, without distraction — and discovering that you are better company than you think. The woman who is comfortable alone is the woman who will never settle out of desperation.

Your twenties are for learning, not for having it figured out. — The pressure to have the career, the relationship, the plan, and the identity locked down by twenty-five is a lie designed to rush you into decisions you're not ready for. Give yourself permission to be in process. The best decisions of your life will come from the lessons your twenties taught you — not from the achievements they produced.

Comparison will steal everything you have. — Her engagement. Her promotion. Her body. Her life. The moment you begin measuring your story against hers, you lose the ability to appreciate your own. Comparison doesn't motivate. It immobilizes. And the woman who escapes it discovers something remarkable: her life, exactly as it is, has a beauty and a purpose that was invisible as long as she was looking at someone else's.

Your faith is the foundation for everything else. — Your career will shift. Your relationships will change. Your body will age. Your circumstances will surprise you. The only thing that doesn't move is the God underneath it all.

Build your faith now — not as a backup plan, but as the primary structure. A woman who builds on faith builds on the only thing strong enough to hold everything else.

Saying yes to everything is saying no to yourself. — Every yes carries a cost — time, energy, margin, peace. And a woman who cannot say no will eventually give away every resource she has, leaving nothing for the things and people that matter most. Learn the power of the strategic no. It will protect your health, your relationships, and your sanity.

Forgiveness is not optional. — You will be hurt. Deeply. Probably more than once. And the temptation will be to carry it — to nurse the wound, to rehearse the offense, to let the bitterness become a companion. Don't. Forgiveness is not a gift to the person who hurt you. It is freedom for the woman who's been carrying the weight. Release it before it becomes your identity.

The right man will not complete you. — He will complement you. He will walk beside you. He will challenge, encourage, and support you. But he will not fill the hole that only God can fill. The woman who enters a relationship looking for a savior will always be disappointed. The woman who enters it already whole will find a partner — not a replacement for the work she was supposed to do herself.

You are not behind. — Not in your career. Not in your relationships. Not in your faith. Not in your life. The world's timeline is not God's timeline. And the woman who stops measuring her pace against the world's calendar discovers something liberating: she is exactly where she is supposed to be — and the next chapter is being written by someone who has never once been late.

List 5: Ten Ways to Be Strong Without Losing Your Softness

Understand that softness is not the opposite of strength — it is the completion of it. — The world will try to tell you that to be strong you must harden. That's a half-truth. A woman who is only hard is brittle — she breaks under pressure. A woman who is strong and soft bends without breaking, absorbs the blow without losing her shape. The combination is not a contradiction. It is the design.

Speak the truth — but speak it with kindness. — You can be direct without being destructive. You can be honest without being harsh. The woman who speaks truth wrapped in kindness delivers a message that lands — because the hearer can receive it without defending against it. Truth without kindness is a weapon. Kindness without truth is flattery. The woman who holds both changes the people around her.

Set boundaries — and enforce them with grace. — A boundary is not a wall. It is a fence with a gate. The woman who sets boundaries is not shutting people out — she is defining where she ends and another begins. And the grace with which she enforces them determines whether the relationship survives the boundary or dies against it. Firmness and gentleness are not enemies. They are partners.

Cry when it hurts — and get back up when it's over. — The strong woman doesn't bypass the tears. She doesn't pretend the pain isn't real. She sits in it. She feels it. She lets it wash over her. And then — when the wave recedes — she stands. Not because she's unaffected. Because she is resilient. Tears and tenacity can live in the same woman. They often do.

Protect the people you love — fiercely and quietly. — Strength in a woman is not always loud. Sometimes it's the text at midnight. The prayer whispered over a sleeping child. The conversation she has with the school. The line she draws that no one sees but everyone benefits from. A woman who protects quietly is a woman whose strength doesn't need an audience.

Carry your pain without transferring it. — A strong woman hurts. But she doesn't pass the hurt to every person she touches. She doesn't punish her children for her bad day. She doesn't wound her husband because she was wounded at work. She processes her pain — in prayer, in community, in her own quiet space — and she comes to the people she loves with what they need, not with the residue of what she's carrying.

Be vulnerable with the right people. — Vulnerability is not weakness. But vulnerability with the wrong people is dangerous. The strong, soft woman knows the difference. She opens her heart to the women who have earned it — the ones who hold her secrets with care, who don't compete with her pain, who listen without fixing. Those women get the real her. Everyone else gets the gracious version.

Fight for others before you fight for yourself. — The strongest women are often the ones whose first instinct is advocacy — for their children, for the voiceless, for the overlooked. This is not self-neglect. It is the overflow of a woman whose strength is outward-facing. She fights for herself too — but her first reflex is to shield the ones who can't shield themselves.

Forgive quickly — but don't forget the lesson. — Forgiveness and memory are not opposites. The soft woman forgives. The strong woman remembers the lesson — not to punish, but to protect. She doesn't hold the grudge. She holds the wisdom. And wisdom without bitterness is one of the most powerful tools a woman can carry.

Kneel before you stand. — The strongest posture a woman can assume is not standing tall. It is kneeling low. The woman who begins on her knees — in prayer, in surrender, in dependence on God — rises with a strength that is not her own. And borrowed strength from the Almighty is more formidable than anything she could manufacture by herself.

List 6: Ten Ways to Be Gentle Without Being a Doormat

Understand that gentleness is a choice, not a default. — A doormat has no choice. It absorbs whatever steps on it because it was placed there to be stepped on. Gentleness is entirely different. It is the deliberate decision to respond with softness when hardness is available. The gentle woman could escalate. She could retaliate. She could wound. She chooses not to — and that choice is the purest expression of strength disguised as grace.

Say no with a soft voice and a firm spine. — Gentleness doesn't mean saying yes to everything. It means saying no without cruelty, without guilt, and without wavering. The gentle woman declines the invitation, corrects the behavior, enforces the boundary — all without raising her voice. And the person on the other end walks away feeling respected, not demolished. That is artistry.

Refuse to absorb what is not yours to carry. — The doormat absorbs everyone's anger, everyone's disappointment, everyone's emotional overflow. The gentle woman does not. She can be present without being a sponge. She can empathize without absorbing. She can love without losing herself. The difference is boundaries — and the gentle woman has them, even if she enforces them quietly.

Confront when necessary — with love, not with fury. — The doormat avoids confrontation because she's afraid of the conflict. The gentle woman engages it because she loves the relationship enough to protect it. "I need to talk to you about something. I love you, and this matters enough to address." That sentence is gentle, brave, and devastatingly effective — because it combines truth with tenderness.

Stop apologizing for existing. — "I'm sorry" has become the soundtrack of the modern woman — for taking up space, for having an opinion, for needing something, for being inconvenient. Stop. You are not an inconvenience. You are a person. Gentleness doesn't require constant apology. It requires the confidence to be present without shrinking.

Let others disagree with you without caving. — A doormat changes her position the moment someone pushes back. A gentle woman holds her ground — not because she can't hear the other perspective, but because she's already considered it and arrived at her conviction. She listens. She nods. She respects. And she stays where she is.

Serve from fullness, not from emptiness. — The doormat serves because she's afraid to stop. The gentle woman serves because she has something to give. The difference is motive — and motive determines whether the serving builds her up or burns her out. A woman who serves from an empty tank is not gentle. She is depleted. Fill the tank first. Then pour.

Protect your dignity. — Gentleness does not require you to tolerate disrespect. The gentle woman can walk away from a conversation that demeans her, a relationship that diminishes her, or a situation that violates her worth — all without rage, all without revenge, all without losing her composure. She simply exits. With dignity intact.

Be soft with the people who are breaking. — The world is full of broken people pretending they're not. The gentle woman sees through the performance. She sits with the grieving. She holds the hand of the anxious. She speaks softly to the child who is acting out because he's hurting inside. This is not weakness. This is ministry — the kind that operates without a microphone and changes lives without anyone noticing.

Remember that Jesus was gentle — and He was anything but weak. — He washed feet. He wept at a graveside. He let children climb into His lap. He spoke tenderly to the woman caught in her shame. And He also flipped tables, rebuked Pharisees, and walked willingly into death. Gentleness and power lived in the same person — and they live in you. You don't have to choose between them. You are designed to carry both.

List 7: Ten Ways to Stop Performing and Start Being

Admit that you've been performing. — The smile that hides the exhaustion. The "I'm fine" that buries the truth. The curated image that masks the chaos. Most women don't even realize they're performing until the performance collapses — and then they wonder why no one saw it coming. Step one: admit the act. Not with shame. With honesty.

Identify who you're performing for. — Your mother? Your friends? The internet? The woman at church who seems to have it all together? Name the audience. Because once you name the audience, you can fire them. Your life was not written for their applause. It was written for an audience of One.

Let someone see the real version. — Not the entire world. One person. Your closest friend. Your husband. Your sister. Say, "Here's what's really going on." That sentence cracks the stage open — and what emerges is not weakness. It is the most authentic version of you. And authentic is what the people who love you have been waiting for.

Stop managing other people's perceptions. — You cannot control what people think of you. You can exhaust yourself trying — adjusting, performing, curating, anticipating. Or you can release it. Let them think what they think. The woman who stops managing perceptions discovers she has energy for things that actually matter.

Let your home be imperfect when people visit. — The dishes in the sink. The toys on the floor. The laundry on the couch. Let them see it. Not as rebellion — as freedom. A woman who opens her imperfect home says, "You are welcome here as I am, and I am not pretending." That invitation is more generous than any spotless living room.

Quit the commitments you took on for image. — The committee you joined to look involved. The volunteer role you accepted to seem generous. The project you said yes to because you were afraid of what they'd think if you said no. If the commitment is rooted in performance rather than calling, it is stealing time from the things you were actually meant to do.

Grieve the version of yourself you've been projecting. — She was impressive. She was exhausting. She was not real. Let her go. Grieve her if you need to — because she represented something you wanted to be. But she was never sustainable. And the real you — the messy, honest, imperfect, faithful you — is the one God is actually working with.

Practice being ordinary. — The quiet Tuesday with nothing to post. The weekend with no plans. The season with no big announcement. Let yourself be ordinary. Ordinariness is not failure. It is the soil where most of life's deepest growth happens — far from the spotlight, far from the performance, far from the applause.

Replace the performance with presence. — Instead of performing for your children, be present with them. Instead of performing at church, worship honestly. Instead of performing for your husband, sit beside him and be real. Presence is the antidote to performance — and it costs nothing but courage.

Ask God to show you who you are without the act. — "God, who am I when the performance stops? Who did You make me to be underneath all of this?" That prayer is the beginning of the truest version of yourself. And the woman who asks it with genuine surrender will discover that the person underneath the act was always the one God loved.

List 8: Ten Standards Every Woman Should Refuse to Lower

Your standard for how you are spoken to. — You are a woman made in the image of God. That means no one — not your boss, not your partner, not your parent, not your child — has the right to speak to you with contempt, cruelty, or degradation. This is not about being oversensitive. It is about refusing to normalize disrespect. The standard is non-negotiable.

Your standard for honesty in relationships. — Half-truths, manipulation, gaslighting, and deception are not inconveniences to tolerate. They are violations of the trust every relationship requires. A woman who tolerates dishonesty in her closest relationships will eventually lose the ability to trust anyone — including herself.

Your standard for purity. — The culture will tell you this standard is outdated. That sexual freedom means no boundaries, no waiting, no moral framework. But the woman who holds her body as sacred — not because she's afraid of her desires, but because she respects their power — is a woman who has understood something the culture hasn't: that purity is not repression. It is stewardship.

Your standard for how you treat others. — Kindness. Respect. Honesty. Grace. Regardless of how others treat you, your standard for how you treat them is a reflection of who you are — not of who they are. The woman who lowers her standard to match someone else's behavior has just let that person dictate her character.

Your standard for what you consume. — The content. The conversations. The media. The relationships. Everything that enters your mind shapes your soul. A woman who consumes without discernment is a woman whose identity is being formed by forces she didn't choose. Guard what you let in. Your standard for consumption is your standard for who you're becoming.

Your standard for your faith. — Not the appearance of faith. Not the performance of faith. The real, daily, costly, honest pursuit of God. A woman who lets her faith devolve into a Sunday habit has lowered the standard that holds every other standard in place.

Your standard for rest. — The world will tell you to keep going. To do more. To rest when you're dead. But God rested — and He was not tired. He was establishing a pattern. A woman who refuses to lower her standard for rest is a woman who will still be standing when the women who refused to rest have collapsed.

Your standard for the legacy you leave. — Every decision you make today is writing a chapter your children and grandchildren will read. A woman who lowers her standards for convenience is writing a story with a weak plot. Hold the standard. Not for perfection. For direction.

Your standard for how you speak about yourself. — The jokes about your body. The casual self-deprecation. The inner monologue that tears you apart. Stop. If you wouldn't let someone else say those words to your daughter, don't say them to yourself. Your standard for self-talk is a mirror of your standard for self-worth.

Your standard for what you settle for. — The job that diminishes you. The relationship that drains you. The friendship that takes without giving. The life that is comfortable but purposeless. A woman who settles is a woman who has decided that what she has is all she deserves. That is a lie. You deserve what God designed for you. And what He designed is never the thing you settle for.

List 9: Ten Ways to Carry Yourself with Quiet Confidence

Walk into every room like you belong there — because you do. — Not with arrogance. With the settled assurance that the God who placed you in this moment has a purpose for your presence. Quiet confidence doesn't announce itself. It arrives — and the room notices without being told.

Speak with fewer words and more intention. — The woman who fills every silence with chatter is performing. The woman who chooses her words deliberately is leading. Say less. Mean more. Let the quality of your speech replace the quantity.

Hold your posture. — Shoulders back. Head high. Eyes level. Not as vanity — as declaration. The body communicates what the mouth doesn't. A woman who carries herself with physical dignity tells the world, without speaking, that she knows her worth.

Refuse to compete. — Quiet confidence doesn't need to win the room. It doesn't compare, jockey, or position. It simply exists — content to be what it is, regardless of what the woman beside it appears to be. Competition is the mark of insecurity. Composure is the mark of peace.

Receive a compliment without deflecting. — "Thank you" is a complete response. Not "Oh, this old thing." Not "No, I look terrible." Not "You're the one who looks amazing." Deflection is a refusal to accept what was offered. A woman with quiet confidence receives it — simply, graciously — and moves on.

Don't chase people who have left. — The friendship that faded. The relationship that ended. The person who chose to walk away. Let them go. A woman with quiet confidence doesn't beg, pursue, or manipulate. She grieves, releases, and trusts that the right people will stay — and the ones who left were never meant to.

Be comfortable with being misunderstood. — Not everyone will get you. Not everyone will agree with you. Not everyone will approve. A woman with quiet confidence doesn't need universal approval. She needs alignment with her values and her God — and everything else is noise.

Admit what you don't know. — "I don't know, but I'll find out" is one of the most confident sentences a woman can speak. It communicates honesty, humility, and competence — all at once. The woman who pretends to know everything reveals insecurity. The woman who admits her gaps reveals strength.

Let your work speak. — Stop narrating your effort. Stop explaining your sacrifice. Stop marketing your contribution. Do the work. Let the results speak. The woman whose output is undeniable doesn't need to advertise it. The evidence is in the room — and quiet confidence lets it stand on its own.

Rest in God's assessment of you. — The world's review is always changing. God's has never changed. You are loved. You are called. You are enough — not because of what you've done, but because of whose you are. A woman who rests in that assessment walks with a confidence that doesn't waver when the world's opinion shifts — because her foundation never does.

List 10: Ten Ways to Stop Apologizing for Who God Made You to Be

Stop apologizing for your strength. — You are not too much. You are not intimidating. You are strong — and strength in a woman is not a flaw to manage. It is a gift to deploy. The world may not know what to do with a strong woman. That is the world's problem, not yours.

Stop apologizing for your emotions. — You feel deeply. That is not weakness. It is capacity — the capacity to grieve, to love, to empathize, to rejoice at a depth that most people will never reach. The woman who apologizes for her tears has been told a lie about what strength looks like. Real strength feels everything and keeps standing.

Stop apologizing for your boundaries. — "No" is not cruel. It is clear. And the people who make you feel guilty for saying it are the people who benefited most from your inability to say it. Your boundaries protect your peace, your time, and your calling. Never apologize for protecting what God entrusted to you.

Stop apologizing for your ambition. — The desire to build, to lead, to create, to excel — this is not unfeminine. It is the image of a creative God expressed through a woman who takes her gifts seriously. Ambition directed by faith is not selfishness. It is stewardship.

Stop apologizing for your voice. — Speak. In the meeting. At the table. In the church. In the marriage. You have things to say that the room needs to hear — and your silence is not humility if it's born from fear. Humility speaks when it's called to. Fear stays quiet when it shouldn't.

Stop apologizing for your past. — You've confessed it. You've grieved it. You've learned from it. It is finished. The woman who keeps apologizing for what God has already forgiven is refusing to accept the gift of grace. Stop rehearsing what He's already released. Walk forward.

Stop apologizing for taking time for yourself. — The bath. The walk. The book. The hour alone. You are not selfish for refueling. You are responsible. A woman who runs on empty pours nothing into anyone. A woman who fills herself first overflows into everything she touches.

Stop apologizing for your appearance. — Your face. Your body. Your age. Your hair. Your features. These are not mistakes. They are the deliberate design of a God who doesn't mass-produce. You are the only one of you. Stop apologizing for what He made on purpose.

Stop apologizing for your faith. — In a world that celebrates everything except the cross, your faith will make people uncomfortable. Let it. The woman who hides her faith to avoid friction has traded her calling for convenience. Stand in it. Openly. Without apology.

Stop apologizing for being you. — The full, unedited, imperfect, becoming, powerful, gentle, faithful, feeling, growing, stumbling, rising version of you. She is not a draft. She is not a mistake. She is the woman God is shaping — and she has nothing to apologize for.

WOMANHOOD & IDENTITY: QUOTES

"For you created my inmost being; you knit me together in my mother's womb." — *Psalm 139:13*

"I praise you because I am fearfully and wonderfully made." — *Psalm 139:14*

"Our identity is not found in our accomplishments, but in being a child of God." — *Priscilla Shirer, The Resolution for Women*

"Charm is deceptive, and beauty is fleeting; but a woman who fears the Lord is to be praised." — *Proverbs 31:30*

"There is no 'my truth' when it comes to God." — *Alisa Childers, Another Gospel?*

"You are altogether beautiful, my darling; there is no flaw in you." — *Song of Solomon 4:7*

"Selfhood, including one's sex, becomes a gift that can be accepted rather than constructed." — Abigail Favale, The Genesis of Gender

"My faith is just my life, it's a part of it." — Candace Cameron Bure, interview

"Let your adorning be the hidden person of the heart, with the imperishable beauty of a gentle and quiet spirit." — Adapted from 1 Peter 3:3-4

"Living original means being confident that God made you in a really cool, unique way." — Sadie Robertson Huff, Live Original

WOMANHOOD & IDENTITY: PUTTING IT INTO PRACTICE

Write your identity statement this week. — In one paragraph, answer: "Who am I — not by what I do, but by who God says I am?" Read it every morning for thirty days. Watch how it rewires your internal monologue.

Identify the three loudest voices defining you right now — and evaluate them. — Write the name of each voice next to the message it's been sending. Then ask: "Does this voice have the authority to define me?" Replace every unauthorized voice with a verse.

Unfollow five accounts this week that make you feel inadequate. — Not with bitterness. With intention. Replace them with accounts that speak truth, encourage growth, and remind you of who you really are.

The next time someone compliments you, say "thank you" — and stop. — No deflecting. No minimizing. No redirecting. Just receive it. Practice this for one full week and notice what shifts.

Write down one thing about yourself you've been apologizing for — and stop. — Your strength. Your voice. Your body. Your emotions. Your faith. Name it. Then make the decision: I will not apologize for what God made on purpose.

Spend twenty minutes this week sitting in silence with no screen, no book, no noise. — Just you and your thoughts. Let them come. Let them pass. Get comfortable with your own company. The woman who can sit with herself is the woman who doesn't need the room to validate her.

Ask one trusted friend this week: "What do you see in me that I might not see in myself?" — Listen to her answer. Write it down. Keep it where you can read it on the days the lie gets loud.

Memorize Psalm 139:14 this week. — "I praise you because I am fearfully and wonderfully made; your works are wonderful, I know that full well." Let it become the wallpaper of your mind.

Do one thing this week that the "not enough" voice told you you couldn't. — Apply for it. Start it. Say it. Build it. Show the voice that its authority is revoked.

Before bed tonight, thank God for three specific things about how He made you. — Not generic gratitude. Specific. "Thank You for the way I love deeply. Thank You for my persistence. Thank You for the way I see people." Specificity is the antidote to the vague lie that says you're not enough.

CATEGORY TWO

Sisterhood

❦

List 1: Ten Marks of a True Friend

She tells you the truth — especially when it's hard. — A true friend is not the woman who tells you what you want to hear. She is the woman who tells you what you need to hear, delivered with enough love that you can receive it. She will say, "That relationship is killing you." She will say, "You're not listening to your husband." She will say, "You are better than this." And she will say it because she would rather risk the friendship than watch you walk off a cliff. That is love with a spine.

She shows up without being asked. — The true friend does not wait for the invitation. She arrives at the hospital before you think to text. She drops off dinner the week after the funeral. She picks up the phone on the third ring when she sees your name. She has a radar for when you're sinking — and she moves toward you before you've built up the nerve to ask. Proximity is her love language.

She keeps your secrets like they are her own. — The things you say to her at midnight do not show up in someone else's conversation the next afternoon. She holds your confessions, your fears, your failures, and the ugly truths you have told no one else — and she carries them with the reverence of a vow. In a world where most friendships leak like sieves, a woman who does not is worth her weight in gold.

She celebrates your wins without envy. — When you announce the promotion, the pregnancy, the book deal, the move — her face lights up. Genuinely. She does not calculate what your gain means for her ranking. She does not wait three days to text a lukewarm congratulations. She cheers loudly, without reservation, and she means it. The woman who can celebrate another woman's success without flinching has mastered the rarest of friendships.

She does not compete with you. — She is not measuring her house against yours. Her body against yours. Her marriage against yours. Her children against yours. She walks beside you, not against you — because she has accepted that her life is hers and yours is yours, and comparison between them is pointless. A true friend is a sister. Sisters share the inheritance. They do not fight over it.

She is safe to be weak in front of. — You don't have to perform with her. You don't have to dress for her. You don't have to apologize for your tears in her presence. You can arrive at her door unwashed, unedited, and undone — and she makes room for all of it. A friend who is safe to be weak in front of is a friend you will keep for life, because the world has too few of those and you know it.

She stays when it stops being convenient. — When you get boring. When you get busy. When you go through the depressive season where you cannot muster the energy to be fun. When you become a mother and disappear for three years. When grief makes you hard to be around. The true friend stays through the inconvenient seasons — because she understood, long before you did, that friendship was never meant to be a transaction.

She brings you back to God. — She is not threatened by your spiritual questions. She is not shaken by your doubts. But she does not leave you in them, either. She reminds you of what you believe when you've forgotten. She prays for you when you cannot pray for yourself. She points you back to the Word when the world has you spinning. A friend whose orbit bends toward Christ pulls you toward Him too.

She apologizes when she is wrong. — She does not need to win every disagreement. She can say, "I was out of line. I'm sorry. Forgive me." Without hedging. Without a defense. Without a subtle reversal that makes it your fault. A friendship in which neither party can apologize cleanly is a friendship that will eventually choke on unspoken resentment. The true friend has mastered the apology that restores.

She is in it for the long haul. — Not a season. Not a friendship that ends when the circumstances change. Not a friendship that fades when you move cities or get married or have children. She is the woman who will still be sitting beside you forty years from now, both of you gray, both of you laughing, both of you astonished at how much life there was between the beginning and the end. That is the friend worth becoming, and the friend worth praying for.

List 2: Ten Kinds of Women to Keep Close

The woman who has walked ahead of you. — Every woman needs a friend who is five, ten, twenty years further down the road. A woman who has already been through the season you are entering. Who knows the marriage you are trying to build, the children you are trying to raise, the career you are trying to navigate — because she has already walked it. Her perspective is a gift. Her experience is a map. Seek her out. Keep her close.

The woman who is walking beside you. — The friend at the same stage. The one with children the same age as yours, in the middle of the same exhaustion, navigating the same questions. She keeps you sane. She reminds you that what you are experiencing is normal, that you are not broken, that the season will pass. The friend at your pace is oxygen in a decade that can feel airless.

The woman who is coming behind you. — The younger friend. The sister a decade your junior. The woman who is where you were five years ago. You need her too — because pouring into someone younger forces you to live what you're trying to teach. She keeps you honest. She keeps you humble. And she gives you the chance to hand down the wisdom someone older once handed to you.

The woman who shares your faith. — There are friendships that can carry the weight of your professional life, your hobbies, your neighborhood. But there are conversations only the sister who prays with you can hold. The friend who shares your faith is the one who understands why the decision feels hard, because she is weighing it the same way you are — through the lens of scripture, not through the lens of culture. She is rare. Build your inner circle around her.

The woman who makes you laugh until you cry. — Do not underestimate this woman. In a life that will hand you enough tears, the friend who can make you laugh — hard, honestly, helplessly — is a gift. She reminds you that joy is still possible. She punctures the seriousness when it starts to suffocate you. She is medicine. Refill the prescription.

The woman who has survived what you fear. — The woman who has buried a spouse. The woman who has lost a child. The woman whose marriage ended. The woman whose diagnosis was bad. If you walk into your own hard season, you need the friend who has walked a worse one — because she knows what no one else can teach you: that you will survive. Her scars are your assurance.

The woman who tells you the truth. — You already read about her in the previous list. Keep her close. Protect her place in your life. In a world full of flatterers, the friend who will say the hard thing is the friend who is actually saving your life — even when the truth stings.

The woman who has time for you. — Some women are too busy to be friends. They are running empires, raising six children, traveling constantly. They may be admirable. They are not available. The friend worth building with is the one who can actually show up — who has the bandwidth to answer the call, sit at the coffee shop, be present when you need her. Time is love. The friend who gives it to you is the friend to keep.

The woman who is honest about her own struggles. — Avoid the friend who is always fine, whose marriage is always perfect, whose children never misbehave, whose life is airbrushed even off the screen. That friendship will eventually drain you — because you will feel the pressure to perform the same illusion. Choose the friend who is honest about her mess. You will rest in her company.

The woman who prays with you. — When she says, "Can I pray for you right now?" — and she means it, right now, in the middle of the parking lot, hand on your shoulder — you have found a kind of friend most women will never have. Her prayers will hold you up on the days you cannot stand. Her prayers will outlast this book, this season, and maybe even this life. Cling to her.

List 3: Ten Kinds of Women to Love From a Distance

The woman who competes with you. — She cannot celebrate your wins. She subtly measures every aspect of her life against yours. She wants to know your salary, your weight, your square footage, your husband's title — not to know you, but to rank herself. Love her. Pray for her. But do not give her access to the soft parts of your life. She will weaponize them.

The woman who cannot keep a confidence. — You told her one thing. You heard it back from someone else two weeks later. That is information you now possess about her — and it is non-negotiable. A woman who leaks is not a woman to build with. Stay friendly. Stay distant. Tell her nothing that you would not publish on a billboard.

The woman who is always the victim. — Every story she tells ends with her being wronged. Every friendship she's had has ended because of someone else. Every job she's lost was someone else's fault. Watch the pattern. If you become her friend, you will eventually become a villain in one of her stories. Keep a respectful distance.

The woman who gossips to you about everyone. — She talks about her coworkers to you. She talks about her sister to you. She talks about her pastor to you. Understand what this means: she is talking about you to someone else. There is no version of her in which you are the exception. Love her. Smile. Offer nothing.

The woman who drains without giving. — Every conversation is about her problems. Every coffee is her processing her life. When it is your turn to share, her eyes drift. Her replies shrink. Friendship is not a spreadsheet, but it is a reciprocal relationship — and the woman who only takes is not a friend. She is an extraction operation disguised as one.

The woman who cannot apologize. — She hurts you. You address it. She turns it around on you. By the end of the conversation, somehow you are apologizing to her. That is not a friendship — that is a manipulation. Love her from a distance. Do not hand her another opportunity to repeat the pattern.

The woman whose worldview will erode yours. — The friend who constantly encourages you to compromise the standards you've set. Who mocks your faith. Who nudges you toward choices you know are wrong. Who rolls her eyes at your boundaries. You do not need to abandon her — but you cannot build your life with her. Her influence will win if you give it enough proximity.

The woman who is hot and cold without warning. — One day she adores you. The next day she is distant, icy, inexplicably wounded. You are constantly recalibrating, apologizing for offenses you did not commit, trying to regain ground you did not lose. This is not friendship. This is emotional weather you cannot predict. Love her gently. Keep your home stable by keeping her outside of it.

The woman who demands, rather than invites. — Her needs are urgent. Your needs are inconvenient. She expects your time, your energy, your emotional availability — on her schedule, at her volume. Friendship is not a subscription service. The woman who demands you is the woman whose demands will expand every year. Love her. Limit her.

The woman who tempts you back to who you used to be. — The friend from the life you have left behind. The one who keeps reminding you of the version of yourself you are trying not to be. The one who wants a drinking partner, a gossip partner, a partner in the old patterns. You are not obligated to rebuild that friendship on new terms if she refuses to acknowledge new terms exist. Love her from a distance. Mourn what was. Walk on.

List 4: Ten Ways to Show Up When She's Falling Apart

Come without being invited. — She will not ask. Most women who are falling apart cannot find the words to ask. They cannot find their phone. They cannot form the sentence. You do not wait for the invitation. You show up — to the door, to the hospital, to the kitchen. You arrive, and you stay.

Do not say, "Let me know if you need anything." — That sentence is beautiful and useless. It transfers the labor to the woman who is drowning. Replace it with specifics. "I'm bringing dinner Tuesday at six. What allergies do your kids have?" "I'll pick up your groceries this weekend. Send me your list." "I'll be at your house at ten on Thursday to do your laundry." Specific offers are received. Vague offers are declined.

Bring something that doesn't need a thank-you note. — A meal she doesn't have to return the dish for. A gift card with no expiration. A bag of groceries on the porch. She has nothing left to give right now — not even a thank-you. Remove the obligation. Love her without a receipt.

Sit with her in the silence. — Do not feel the need to fill it. Do not offer a Bible verse in the first ten minutes. Do not try to fix her pain with your words. Sometimes the most powerful thing a friend can do is sit — hand in hand, tea on the table, no explanation required. Presence is the ministry. Your mouth can stay closed.

Listen without immediately redirecting to yourself. — Resist the reflex to say, "That happened to me once, too." This is her moment, not yours. She does not need your parallel story. She needs your ears. Let her talk. Let her cry. Let her repeat the same story three times if she needs to. You are there to absorb, not to compare.

Ask about the specifics. — "How are you?" is hard to answer when you are falling apart. Better: "How was last night?" "Did you sleep?" "Did you eat today?" "Is there someone I can call for you?" Specific questions are easier to answer — and they communicate that you are paying attention to her actual life, not to her performance of being okay.

Do the boring, invisible work. — Fold her laundry. Do her dishes. Walk her dog. Take her car to the mechanic. Pick up her prescriptions. These things are not glamorous. They do not make a good photo. They are the exact things she cannot do right now — and the friend who does them is the friend who is actually loving her.

Do not give advice she didn't ask for. — Unless she explicitly asks, "What should I do?" — your advice is unwanted, even when it's good. She is not ready to plan yet. She is still feeling. Advice too early is not help; it is a subtle way of telling her to stop feeling so you can stop feeling awkward. Let her feel. Love her there.

Check on her again — after the crisis has passed. — Everyone shows up the first week. Very few people show up the sixth month. The texts stop. The meals stop. And she is left alone, still grieving, surrounded by silence. Be the friend who texts at month three. Month six. Year one. That sustained presence is the love that actually heals.

Pray for her when she cannot pray for herself. — There will be seasons where she cannot open her Bible, cannot form a prayer, cannot feel God's nearness. Stand in the gap. Pray her name out loud to the Lord. Intercede for her by name. When she tells you, a year later, that she couldn't pray and didn't know how she made it — you will know. Your prayers carried her.

List 5: Ten Conversations Every Woman Should Have With Her Closest Friends

The conversation about what you fear. — Not the polite fears. The real ones. The fear that you will be alone forever. The fear that your marriage won't last. The fear that your children will reject you. The fear that you will never be enough. Name them. Out loud. To someone who will not flinch. Fear named in the light loses most of its power.

The conversation about your money. — What you have. What you owe. What you spend. What you're saving for. What you can't afford. Money is one of the last taboos of female friendship — and that silence keeps women isolated, ashamed, and alone with their financial fears. The friendship that can talk honestly about money is the friendship that can talk honestly about anything.

The conversation about your marriage. — Not the curated version. The real one. The hard weeks. The loneliness. The conflicts that keep recurring. The seasons you don't like your husband very much. This is not gossip about him. This is the sacred space where a trusted friend holds your marriage gently and helps you remember what is worth fighting for.

The conversation about your faith struggles. — The prayers that go unanswered. The doubts you cannot shake. The passages you don't understand. The church experience that wounded you. A friend who is safe to doubt with is a friend who will help you find your way back to belief — not by shaming you out of your questions, but by walking through them with you.

The conversation about your body. — What it's doing. What's changed. What hurts. What you are grieving about it. The weight. The aging. The scars. The infertility. The illness. Female friendship at its best is the one place a woman can be honest about her body without being reduced to it.

The conversation about your past. — The version of you before she knew you. The mistakes. The failures. The season you are still a little ashamed of. The real friend will receive all of it — and she will not see you differently afterward. She will see you more fully. And being fully seen by someone who still loves you is one of the deepest experiences a human can have.

The conversation about what you want. — Not what is expected of you. Not what your mother wanted. Not what your husband hopes you'll do. What do you want? What dream have you been quietly carrying that you have not told anyone? Name it. The friend who helps you say it out loud helps you bring it into the world.

The conversation about how she has hurt you. — The moment she said the wrong thing. The time she wasn't there. The subtle pattern that has been bothering you for a year. Say it. With grace. With clarity. The friendship that can survive a hard conversation is the friendship that actually becomes deep. The friendships that cannot survive it were not as deep as you thought.

The conversation about aging. — The parents getting older. The bodies getting slower. The kids growing up. The seasons ending. The woman in the mirror who looks like her mother now. This is a conversation the younger culture cannot have — but your closest friend, the one aging beside you, can.

The conversation about dying. — Yes. Really. What do you want your daughters to know? What prayer do you want spoken over you? What do you want on your headstone? What do you hope will still be standing a hundred years after you are gone? The friend who can talk about death is the friend who is actually helping you live.

List 6: Ten Ways to Confront Without Destroying

Go to her in private first. — Not in a group. Not on a text thread. Not in a subtly worded social media post. Face to face. Door closed. Just the two of you. This is not negotiable. The matthew eighteen principle is ancient and correct: the confrontation that begins privately is the one that has a chance of ending reconciled. The confrontation that begins publicly almost never does.

Begin with your love for her. — "I love you. Our friendship matters to me. That is why I am bringing this up." That opening disarms her before you address the hard thing. She hears that her security is not in question. She hears that you are not there to end the friendship — you are there to protect it. That framing changes everything.

Speak from your experience, not her motive. — Say, "When this happened, I felt hurt." Do not say, "You meant to hurt me." You do not know her motive. You know your experience. A confrontation that speaks from your experience is a confrontation she can engage. A confrontation that accuses her of malice is a confrontation she has to defend against.

Be specific. Do not generalize. — "You always do this" is a losing sentence. "Last Tuesday, when you said this, in front of those people — that hurt me" is a sentence she can actually address. Specificity is respect. Generalization is ambush. Always choose specificity.

Leave room for her side. — After you've said what you needed to say, stop. Ask her, "How did you see it?" — and actually listen. She may have context you didn't have. She may have been going through something you didn't know about. She may have been misunderstood. You are not a prosecutor making a case. You are a friend trying to restore.

Expect some defensiveness — and don't take it personally. — No one loves being confronted. Even the most mature woman will have a moment of defensiveness. Breathe. Don't escalate. Give her space to process. The defensiveness is usually the first wave, and it passes if you don't fight it. Underneath it, most people actually want to make things right.

Ask for what you need going forward. — Don't just identify the problem. Name the solution. "Going forward, when this situation comes up, I need X." That sentence gives her a clear path to repair — and it protects the friendship from a repeat offense. Without that sentence, even a good confrontation leaves you back where you started.

Forgive before she asks. — The moment she apologizes — the moment she even leans toward an apology — forgive. Do not make her grovel. Do not extract extra emotional labor. Do not use her apology as a weapon for the next six months. A woman who forgives generously is a woman others will trust to confront them, because they know the confrontation is safe.

Don't rehearse the offense to others. — Once you have addressed it with her, it is finished. You do not take the story to your other friends. You do not keep a running ledger. If the friendship is restored, the offense is buried with the apology. Any woman who resurrects a settled offense is a woman who never really forgave.

Leave the door open — or close it gracefully. — Some confrontations restore the friendship. Some reveal that the friendship cannot be restored. Both outcomes are valid. If she receives the confrontation well, rebuild. If she cannot, release her with dignity. You do not have to make an enemy. But you do not have to keep building on a foundation she refuses to repair.

List 7: Ten Ways to Build Trust That Lasts Decades

Be reliable in small things. — Show up when you said you would. Return the text. Keep the lunch date. Send the card you said you'd send. Trust is not built in grand gestures. It is built in the accumulation of small, consistent, unremarkable reliabilities — which, over decades, become the scaffolding of a friendship that cannot be shaken.

Keep her secrets without exception. — There is no scenario in which it is okay to share what she told you in confidence — not with your husband, not with your mother, not with the friend she has never met. Her confession is hers. You are its keeper. A single breach of that trust can break a friendship that took twenty years to build.

Remember the details of her life. — Her husband's name. Her children's birthdays. The surgery she had. The job interview last Thursday. Send the text the morning of the hard thing. Remember. The woman who remembers is the woman who is actually paying attention — and attention, sustained over decades, is love.

Stay present through her unimpressive seasons. — The friendship built during a trip, a wedding, a crisis is exciting. But the friendship that lasts is the one that endures the unimpressive Tuesdays — the ordinary weeks when nothing is happening, when there is nothing to post about, when she is just living her small life and you are just living yours. Presence in the unremarkable is the proof of a real friendship.

Be generous with credit. — Tell other people what she has done. Brag about her when she is not in the room. Say, "My friend did this — isn't that amazing?" A woman who spreads credit generously builds a reputation that follows her — and her friends want to stay in her orbit because being there makes them feel seen, not diminished.

Show up to the hard things you don't want to show up to. — The funeral. The hospital. The divorce hearing. The rehab visit. The conversation you would rather skip. These are the moments that forge a lifelong bond — and the woman who refuses to skip them earns the kind of trust that nothing else can produce.

Forgive the small offenses without mentioning them. — She forgot your birthday. She was short with you on the phone. She canceled last minute. Let it go. Do not keep a scorecard. Ten years of small forgivenesses produce a friendship that can survive the inevitable big offense. Ten years of small resentments produce a friendship that will eventually break on an unrelated fault line.

Speak well of her husband. — Unless there is abuse — in which case, address it directly — never disparage her husband. Not in jest. Not in frustration. Not ever. Her marriage is not your therapy topic. If you

undermine him in her mind, you are damaging the foundation of her life —
even if she laughs with you in the moment.

Be honest about your own struggles. — Trust is reciprocal. If you never
share your own mess, she will not feel safe sharing hers. A friendship that
lasts is a friendship in which both women have opened up, been received,
and not been destroyed. Your vulnerability is an invitation she will accept.

Choose her repeatedly over decades. — Friendships are not auto-renewing.
They require re-selection. Every year, choose her again. Invest in her again.
Decide, again, that she is worth the time. The woman who chooses her
friends intentionally — year after year — ends up, at seventy, surrounded
by women she has been loving for half a century. That is not luck. That is
harvest.

List 8: Ten Things to Stop Saying About Other Women

"She must think she's better than everyone." — You do not know what she
thinks. You are attributing a motive to a woman who has not told you her
motive — and you are doing it to protect your own insecurity. Stop.
Celebrate her confidence. It is not an indictment of yours.

"She's a lot." — Meaning: she has big energy, big opinions, big feelings, big
presence. We do not say this about men. We say this about women who
take up space in a way that makes us uncomfortable. Examine why you are
uncomfortable. It is usually your problem, not hers.

"She's just doing that for attention." — Another woman's joy, celebration,
or accomplishment is not a cry for attention. It is her life. Your
interpretation of it as attention-seeking says more about the shape of your
own unmet longing than it does about her. Let her post. Let her celebrate.
Let her be.

"She's aged." — Yes. Like every other human being on the planet. Aging is
not a flaw. It is evidence that she is alive. A woman who comments on
another woman's aging is a woman who has absorbed the lie that a woman's
value expires. Refuse the lie. Refuse to pass it on.

"She doesn't have to work." — The assumption that another woman's circumstances are enviable, easy, or undeserved is almost always wrong. You do not know what her life costs her. You do not know what she gave up to have what she has. You do not know what she is carrying that you cannot see. Stop grading her life from the outside.

"She's lucky." — Usually a word women use to diminish another woman's accomplishments without denying them outright. Her body, her marriage, her career, her children — these are not lottery winnings. They are the result of thousands of choices, many of which you did not see her make. Replace "lucky" with "faithful," "disciplined," or "blessed" — and notice how it changes the conversation in your own mind.

"I can't believe she wore that." — Unless she wore a swastika, let her wear it. Her clothing choices are not yours to rank, approve, or ridicule. The woman who critiques what other women wear has turned her friendships into a runway — and she has forgotten that real sisterhood does not keep score on hemlines.

"She's so skinny — she must be starving herself." — Or she's a naturally thin woman. Or she's recovering from an illness. Or she has a thyroid condition. Or she is struggling with an eating disorder and your comment is the last thing she needs. Stop commenting on other women's bodies. In any direction.

"She's so big — why doesn't she take care of herself?" — Same rule. Her body is not your business. She may be in a season of grief, medication, hormonal change, or postpartum. She may be exactly where she's supposed to be. The woman who makes another woman's body her moral commentary is a woman who has forgotten that compassion is more powerful than critique.

"She brought it on herself." — Sometimes women suffer because of their own choices. Sometimes they don't. You usually do not know which one it is. And even when you do, the response is not condemnation — it is compassion, with truth delivered privately. The woman who announces, publicly, that another woman's pain is deserved is a woman who has lost the plot of what a sister is for.

List 9: Ten Rules for Sisterhood in the Age of the Screen

Don't let the screen replace the conversation. — A text is not a friendship. A comment on her post is not a check-in. A like is not love. The screen is a supplement to sisterhood, not a substitute for it. If your closest friendships have been reduced to digital interactions, the friendships are thinner than you realize. Pick up the phone. Meet in person. Let the screen do what it's actually for.

Don't compare her highlight reel to your actual life. — What she posts is not what she lives. The vacation photo is two minutes of a twelve-day trip. The smiling family portrait is the thirtieth attempt after nine meltdowns. The kitchen photo doesn't show the pile of mail in the other room. A woman who measures her real life against another woman's curated one will always lose — because the comparison is not between two lives. It is between a life and a performance.

Don't mistake her silence online for distance. — Some of the best friends are the ones who don't post much. They are not distant. They are living. The woman whose life is too full to document isn't a worse friend — she's often a better one. Do not assume lack of online presence equals lack of love.

Don't air grievances on a platform. — If you have something to say to her, say it to her. In person. In private. The vaguely worded post that is clearly about her — that is not confrontation. That is cowardice dressed in hashtags. Women who do this are not handling conflict. They are advertising it.

Don't turn her wedding, her pregnancy, her loss into your content. — Her major life moments belong to her. You do not get to post about her miscarriage before she has. You do not get to announce her engagement before her family knows. You do not get to narrate her experiences on your timeline. Respect the boundary. Her story is not your material.

Don't let the comment section replace the dinner table. — The quick reply. The thumbs-up. The fire emoji. These are not ways of knowing someone. You cannot substitute a hundred likes a year for one honest conversation. The friendships that endure are the ones that leave the screen.

Don't absorb her anxiety, her outrage, or her doom-scroll. — Some friends will pipe the worst of the internet directly into your group chat — every outrage, every conspiracy, every catastrophe. This is not friendship. It is anxiety contagion. You are allowed to mute her. You are allowed to set boundaries around what comes into your phone. Your peace is worth more than her real-time commentary.

Don't measure a friendship by who texted last. — Keeping score on whose turn it is to reach out is a teenage pattern you can lay down. Some friendships breathe in and out. Some months you carry it. Some months she does. A woman who is counting text messages is a woman who is misreading what sisterhood is actually for.

Don't screenshot her private words to pass to others. — The private conversation is private. A screenshot that breaks that trust — even among your other friends — is a betrayal that cannot be walked back. Treat her private messages like letters addressed to you alone. Because that is what they are.

Don't let the algorithm pick your closest friends. — The women who appear most often on your feed are not necessarily the women who matter most in your life. The algorithm is optimizing for engagement, not intimacy. Choose your closest friends deliberately. Love them beyond the feed. Let the algorithm serve the friendship — never define it.

List 10: Ten Ways to Be the Friend You Wish You Had

Initiate. — Stop waiting to be invited. Stop waiting to be pursued. Be the woman who texts first, plans first, shows up first. The friend you wish you had — the one who reaches out, checks in, organizes the dinner — she is not waiting for you. She is already doing it. Become her. The friendship ecosystem improves when more women initiate.

Remember. — The birthday. The anniversary. The anniversary of the miscarriage. The surgery date. The job interview. Put them in your calendar. Set the reminder. Send the text. Most women do not have one friend who remembers the specific hard days — be the one who does. That memory, expressed, is one of the most loving things a friend can do.

Apologize first. — When there is tension, be the one who goes to her. Do not wait for her to come. The woman who apologizes first — even when the offense was fifty-fifty — is the woman who keeps her friendships alive for decades. Pride is what ends friendships. Humility is what preserves them.

Keep her secrets like they are carved in stone. — Be the kind of friend who is so trustworthy, other women test it and can't find a crack. Be the one she can tell anything to. That reputation is sacred — and it is built one conversation at a time, over years, by never once betraying what you were told.

Celebrate wildly. — Not lukewarmly. Not politely. Wildly. When she announces the thing, lose your mind for her. Send the flowers. Write the card. Show up with cake. Friendships that celebrate well produce women who feel deeply known. Friendships that celebrate weakly produce women who feel quietly lonely even when they are winning.

Confront with love. — Be the friend who has the courage to say the hard thing — gently, privately, without accusation. You have read about this. Now become her. The woman who can deliver a hard truth with love is the woman whose friendships go deeper than almost anyone else's.

Show up at the things you'd rather skip. — The funeral in another state. The baby shower when you're exhausted. The birthday party when your feet hurt. The hospital visit. Be the friend who shows up, even when she didn't expect you to. That kind of consistency is rare. It is what distinguishes friends from acquaintances.

Be honest about yourself. — Go first with vulnerability. Tell her the hard thing in your life before she tells you hers. That modeling gives her permission to do the same. Friendships move at the pace of the bravest woman in them. Be the bravest.

Forgive generously and fully. — Do not carry grudges. Do not keep a private ledger of offenses. Do not bring up old wounds in new fights. A friend who forgives completely is a friend others will trust with everything. Small forgivenesses, consistently given, produce extraordinary friendships.

Keep showing up — for decades. — This is the one that almost nobody does. Stay. Stay when it's convenient. Stay when it isn't. Stay through moves, marriages, babies, divorces, illnesses, seasons of depression, careers that shift, faith that wavers and returns. The friend you wish you had — the one who has been there for thirty years, who still knows you, who still loves you — the only way to become her is to be her. Start today. Keep going. Fifty years from now, the women you are loving tonight will be the women still loving you.

SISTERHOOD: QUOTES

"A friend loves at all times, and a brother is born for a time of adversity." — Proverbs 17:17

"As iron sharpens iron, so one person sharpens another." — Proverbs 27:17

"Community is a safe place because the people in it are safe." — Jennie Allen, *Find Your People*

"Two are better than one, because they have a good return for their labor." — Ecclesiastes 4:9

"Believe, and the mountains will move." — CeCe Winans, K-LOVE interview

"Faithful are the wounds of a friend; profuse are the kisses of an enemy." — Proverbs 27:6

"Being grateful is what makes you joyful." — Attributed to Ann Voskamp

"Greater love has no one than this: to lay down one's life for one's friends." — John 15:13

"If you surrender everything, He will always have your back." — Lauren Daigle, *Daigle Bites* podcast

SISTERHOOD: PUTTING IT INTO PRACTICE

Reach out this week to one friend you have been meaning to contact. — Not with a vague "we should catch up." With a specific invitation. A time. A place. Put it on the calendar before you hang up. Friendships die in the land of vague intention.

Identify one friend who drains and one who fills — and adjust your calendar accordingly. — Not with cruelty. Not with announcement. Just with wisdom. Give more time to the ones who fill you. Give less to the ones who drain. Notice how your own capacity changes in a month.

Practice remembering. — Pick three friends. Put their birthdays, anniversaries, and one hard date (a miscarriage date, a grief date, a surgery anniversary) in your calendar. Send a text on each. Watch how the friendship deepens within a year.

Have one hard conversation this month. — With a friend you have been avoiding. About something that has been bothering you. In person. In love. Without rehearsing her response. Just do it. Most of these conversations go better than you think.

Celebrate one friend publicly this week. — Send her flowers. Post about her. Tell her in a handwritten note what she means to you. Do it for no reason. Generosity without occasion is the most memorable kind.

Stop speaking about another woman in a way you would not say to her face. — For one week. Notice how often the impulse arises. Notice how the absence of that speech changes your inner tone toward the women in your life.

Invite someone younger into your orbit. — Take a woman ten years your junior to coffee. Mentor her, without announcing you are mentoring her. The friendships that change generations are built across generations.

Send a text to a friend mid-crisis saying, "I'm bringing dinner Thursday at 6. What's a food you don't want?" — Specific. Unasked. Non-negotiable. She will cry. Do it anyway.

Pray for one friend by name this week, out loud. — Not "God bless my friends." Her name. Her specific situation. Her husband. Her children. The thing she is facing. Then tell her you prayed. That text alone can change the trajectory of her week.

Write down the names of three friends you want to be sitting beside at seventy. — Then work backward. What do you need to invest in those friendships, starting now, to still be there in forty years? That is not a sentimental exercise. That is strategy for the most important relationships of your life.

CATEGORY THREE

Motherhood

❧

List 1: Ten Things Every Mother Needs to Know Before She Starts

You will not do it perfectly. Stop trying. — The moment you accept that you will fail your children in some way, every day, is the moment you become free to actually mother them. The perfect mother does not exist. She has never existed. She is an invention of a culture that wanted to sell you something. The mother your children actually need is the imperfect, present, honest, repenting, faithful one. Be her.

Your children will reveal things in you you didn't know were there. — Your impatience. Your rage. Your insecurity. Your unhealed wounds from your own childhood. They will surface because your children have a gift for pressing on the exact bruise you didn't know you had. This is not a problem. It is the invitation. Motherhood will sanctify you if you let it — by exposing the things in you that still need to be handed over to God.

You are raising a person, not a project. — Your child is not a report card you are building. Not a trophy you are polishing. Not a reflection of your success. She is a whole person, made in the image of God, with her own calling and her own will. Your job is not to produce a particular outcome. Your job is to point her to the Father, pray for her daily, and love her through every version of herself she will go through on the way to adulthood.

You cannot pour what you do not have. — The mother running on four hours of sleep, two cups of coffee, and resentment is not mothering — she is surviving, and her children can feel the difference. You are not being selfish when you protect your rest, your prayer life, your friendships, your marriage. You are being strategic. The mother who refills her own cup has something to pour out. The mother who doesn't, doesn't.

Your husband is your partner, not your assistant. — Do not parent alone while married. Do not manage everything, schedule everything, remember everything, and then resent him for not helping. Hand him ownership, not tasks. Let him parent his way, not your way. Your children need a mother and a father — not a mother running a household with a male intern.

Comparison will destroy you. — Her children sleep through the night. Yours don't. Her toddler is reading. Yours is still pointing. Her teenager got into Stanford. Yours is figuring out community college. The moment you begin ranking your children against another woman's children, you lose the ability to see the children in front of you. Every child is on a different path. Tend your own.

Screens are not your friend. — The hours you will hand your children over to the screen are hours you cannot get back. The device is not babysitting them — it is shaping them, and the shaping is not benign. Be the mother who is hard on this. Your kids will complain. They will complain more, later, if you weren't.

The early years feel long. The whole thing is short. — There is a Tuesday in February, six years in, when you will want to scream from the monotony. There is also a graduation day that will arrive faster than you can process. Both of these are true. The mother who understands this lives in the long days and the short years simultaneously — present in the grind, aware of the fleeting.

You are not alone. — Every feeling you have had, another mother has had. Every failure you have committed, another mother has committed. The isolation of modern motherhood is one of its cruelest features, and it is largely a lie. Find the women. Tell them the truth. Let them hold you up. Every generation of mothers before you had a village. You have to build yours on purpose — but it exists.

You are going to matter. — Whatever else is said about your life, your role in the formation of these children will be one of the most consequential things you ever do. Not because you controlled outcomes. Because you handed them a framework — a faith, a love, a set of standards — that will echo through their lives long after you are gone. This is the most important work most women will ever do. Take it seriously. But do not take it grimly. Take it with joy.

List 2: Ten Lies the Culture Tells Mothers

"The mother you are during the first year will set everything." — It won't. You are not ruining your child by being exhausted. You are not destroying their development because you put them in the swing so you could shower. Your child's long-term wellbeing is not determined by the perfection of the first twelve months. It is determined by decades of sustained, imperfect love. Breathe.

"You should enjoy every moment." — No. You will not. Some moments are brutal. Some moments are tedious. Some moments are heartbreaking. You will enjoy many moments — and you will survive others. The culture that demands you enjoy every moment has produced a generation of mothers who feel defective because they are honest about how hard it is. Stop pretending.

"You need to be more than a mother." — This lie has two forms. One version tells you that motherhood alone is beneath you — that you need a career, an identity, a platform to be complete. The other tells you that you should be a mother and a career and a platform and a body and a home and a volunteer, all at once. Both lies exhaust women. Motherhood, done well, is more than enough. It is also not the only thing you are. You get to choose the season. You do not have to do everything at once.

"Good mothers never lose their temper." — You will. You will apologize. You will model repair. And that repair will teach your children more than the absence of conflict ever could. A mother who loses her temper and then says, "I was wrong. Forgive me. I love you" is teaching her children how to be humans in real relationships. A mother who pretends she never fails is teaching them something more dangerous — that love requires perfection.

"Your career is a betrayal of your children." — It isn't. Women worked throughout human history — in the fields, in the markets, in the home-based trades, in the family businesses. The stay-at-home, no-outside-work model of motherhood is a relatively recent invention, largely mid-twentieth-century, largely middle-class. There is nothing more spiritual about either model. There is only what is right for your family in your season. Make the choice. Stop apologizing for it either way.

"Your children are a reflection of you." — They are not. They are separate people with their own wills, their own choices, their own rebellions. The parable of the prodigal son is a parable of a perfect Father with a wandering son. If God Himself has children who walk away from Him, the idea that your child's behavior is a mirror of your mothering is theologically naive — and practically cruel. You do your job. They make their choices. Release them to God.

"Breast is best. Bottle is best. Homemade is best. Organic is best." — The mommy-wars industrial complex has produced endless lies dressed as guidance. Some of the loudest voices are not mothers. They are marketers. Do what works for your family. Ignore the rest. Your child's wellbeing is not dependent on which brand of applesauce you chose.

"Attachment parenting will ruin them. Independence parenting will ruin them." — Whatever you are doing, someone on the internet is writing an essay about how it will ruin your children. Tune it out. The vast majority of children raised by loving, attentive, imperfect parents turn out fine. The details of the philosophy matter far less than the presence of the love.

"Your worth goes up when they succeed, and down when they don't." — You are not your child's outcome. Your worth was established before they were born. A mother whose self-image rises and falls with her child's performance has put her identity in the wrong place — and the child feels the pressure, even when she cannot name it. Let your children succeed or fail without making your soul dependent on which one it is.

"You are ruining them." — This is the voice that shows up at three in the morning. After the yelling. After the exhausted shortcut. After the moment you wished you hadn't missed. Hear it — and dismiss it. You are not ruining them. You are raising them. The God who has your children in His hands is bigger than your worst mothering moment. Confess what needs to be confessed. Repair what needs to be repaired. And walk forward.

List 3: Ten Ways to Raise a Daughter Who Knows Her Worth

Tell her she is loved before you tell her she is pretty. — The first word out of your mouth to her should not be about her appearance. Tell her she is loved. Tell her she is a child of God. Tell her she is brave, kind, and clever. The world will comment on her appearance for the rest of her life. Your job is to give her a foundation that is deeper than her face.

Praise her effort, not just her results. — The world will praise her when she wins and go quiet when she doesn't. Be the opposite. Be the mother who notices how hard she tried, how long she practiced, how many times she got back up. That framing will shape how she handles the inevitable failures of adult life — because she will have learned that her worth is in the striving, not in the scoreboard.

Let her see you handle your body with respect. — Do not call yourself fat in front of her. Do not skip meals and tell her you're not hungry. Do not obsess over the scale while claiming you want her to have a healthy body image. Your daughter is watching. She will absorb the relationship you have with your body and replicate it. Model the relationship you want her to inherit.

Teach her the difference between a boundary and a wall. — She will need boundaries her entire life — with men, with friends, with coworkers, with the culture. Teach her, young, that she has the right to say no. That she does not owe anyone an explanation for protecting herself. And teach her, equally, that walls keep good people out. The woman who knows the difference walks through life open but not vulnerable, loving but not absorbed.

Let her see you in the Word. — Not as a performance. As a rhythm. When she walks into the kitchen in the morning and sees your Bible open, she is receiving something the culture cannot replicate. She is seeing a grown woman rooting her identity in scripture — and that image will become her template when she is twenty-five and trying to decide what kind of woman she wants to be.

Talk to her about the screen before the screen talks to her. — The algorithm will find her. The filters will find her. The influencers selling her new ways to hate her body will find her. You cannot prevent that — but you can get there first. Talk honestly. Explain what the algorithm is optimizing for. Help her see it for what it is. A daughter who understands the manipulation is a daughter with some armor against it.

Let her fail — and sit with her in the failure. — Do not rescue every disappointment. Do not solve every problem. Let her experience the normal, small, age-appropriate failures of childhood and adolescence — and be the mother who sits with her afterward, who helps her find the lesson, who reminds her that failure is not the end. A daughter who has been rescued from every hard thing becomes a woman who cannot handle one.

Speak to her about men honestly. — Do not demonize men as a category. Do not romanticize them either. Tell her the truth: that there are men worth her trust and men who will waste her life, and that she will need discernment to tell the difference. Teach her to watch how a man treats his mother, his sisters, the waitress, the woman who can't do anything for him. Those are the tells.

Let her see you love her father well. — The most important thing you can do to shape her future marriage is not a lecture. It is the daily witness of watching you love her father. If she grows up seeing a woman who respects, encourages, and enjoys her husband — while also standing up to him when it matters — she will carry that template into her own marriage. If she sees the opposite, she will carry that one too.

Pray for her out loud, with her. — Not just over her while she sleeps, though do that too. Pray with her. Let her hear you asking God for her future, her heart, her husband, her faith. She will know, from the time she is young, that she has a mother who is fighting for her in prayer — and that awareness will carry her through the years when she is too far away for you to reach with your hands.

List 4: Ten Ways to Raise a Son Who Respects Women

Let him see how you expect to be treated. — He is learning, from age three, what it means to speak to a woman. What it means to interrupt her, ignore her, dismiss her — or to honor her, listen to her, make space for her. Your expectations in your own home are his education. If you let him speak to you with contempt at seven, he will speak to his wife with contempt at thirty.

Teach him that women are not decoration. — The culture will sell him a steady feed of women as bodies, as objects, as accessories. You are competing with that feed every day. Speak about women, in his presence, as full people — professionals, thinkers, athletes, neighbors, leaders. Let him see you treat women, in your life, as full people. He is learning what a woman is from how the adults around him refer to women.

Let him see men in your life treat women well. — His father. His grandfather. His uncles. The men in your church. He is looking for a template — and if he finds one, he will use it. Curate the male presence around him with the same intention you would curate his diet. Put him around men who treat women with respect. Remove him from men who don't.

Teach him to open doors, stand up when she enters, offer his seat. — These are small, old-fashioned habits that have been mocked by the culture. Teach them anyway. Not because women are helpless. Because the habit of noticing a woman — of making room for her, of deferring to her — trains the inner posture toward women that everything else builds on. The small habits become the large instinct.

Give him honest, age-appropriate answers about bodies and sex. — He will get information somewhere. If not from you, from the screen. From the other boys. From content that will shape his view of sex and women in ways you will spend a decade undoing. Be the voice that gets there first. Be awkward. Be specific. Give him a framework rooted in dignity and covenant — because if you don't, the culture will give him one rooted in consumption.

Teach him to handle his emotions without taking them out on women. — Boys who are not allowed to feel become men who explode. Men who explode become husbands who wound. Do not shame his tears. Do not dismiss his fears. Help him name his emotions and process them — because the man who can handle his own interior is the man who does not need a woman to absorb it for him.

Do not let him interrupt, dismiss, or talk over his sisters. — The dynamics that begin at the dinner table at seven become the dynamics of his adult life. If his sister is speaking, he waits. If his sister is hurt, he apologizes. You are not over-correcting — you are setting the floor for how he will treat every woman he encounters for the rest of his life.

Model apology in the home. — Let him see men apologize. Let him hear his father say, "I was wrong. I'm sorry." to his wife and to his children. A boy who has never seen a man apologize will grow into a man who cannot. The apology modeled at home becomes the apology he offers his wife twenty years from now — or not.

Teach him that his strength is for protection, not domination. — As he grows physically, he will become stronger than the women around him. That is biology. What he does with that strength is character. Teach him — explicitly, repeatedly — that his physical power is to be used to protect the weaker, not to intimidate them. That a man who lays hands on a woman in anger has surrendered his right to be called a man.

Pray that he will marry a woman worthy of him — and be a man worthy of her. — Pray for his future wife by name, though you do not know her name. Pray for her protection. Pray for her family. Pray that both of them will arrive at each other having done the work that makes marriage possible. A mother who prays this prayer for twenty years before a wedding is a mother who has moved mountains her son will never see.

List 5: Ten Things to Say to Your Children Every Week

"I'm proud of you." — Not because of an achievement. Because of who they are. Let the sentence stand alone. Let it land. Children who hear "I'm proud of you" without qualifier carry that phrase into their interior for decades.

"I see how hard you're trying." — The world will notice outcomes. Be the voice that notices effort. The child who knows her mother sees her striving does not need to collapse when the striving doesn't produce the outcome.

"I love you." — Of course. But say it out loud, every day, face to face, when nothing else is happening. Not only at bedtime. Not only after the tantrum. Before the moment. For no reason. Make it the atmosphere of your home.

"I was wrong. I'm sorry." — When you were. Model it. Let your child watch you repair. A child who has been apologized to by her mother grows into an adult who knows apology is not shameful.

"Tell me more." — When she starts telling you about her day — about the thing at recess, about the boy she likes, about the book she read — resist the reflex to advise, redirect, or close. Say, "Tell me more." That sentence opens the door wider. It is one of the most generous things a mother can say.

"What do you think?" — Ask for their opinion. On small things first — what color to paint the room, what to have for dinner, what movie to watch. And then, slowly, on bigger things. A child whose opinion is asked for is a child who learns she has a mind worth consulting.

"I believe in you." — At the moment she is afraid she might fail. Before the audition. Before the test. Before the hard conversation. Say it. Mean it. Those four words have launched more confident children into adulthood than any program ever will.

"I'm here. I'm not going anywhere." — When the hard thing happens. When she has made the bad choice. When she is afraid she has used up your love. Say this sentence. Repeat it. A child whose mother's presence is unconditional is a child who will not have to spend her adult life trying to earn love.

"God loves you even more than I do." — Anchor her, from the earliest ages, in the idea that her worth did not begin with your love. It began with God's. Your love is real — but it is a reflection of a larger one. She needs to know that love, because your love will have limits and His will not.

"I like who you are becoming." — Not just who she is. Who she is becoming. That sentence acknowledges that she is in motion — that you are watching her grow, and that the growth itself is what you admire. Children who feel watched approvingly become adults who are not terrified of being seen.

List 6: Ten Things Never to Say to Your Children

"You're just like your father." — As an insult. Never. Your child is half of her father. You cannot insult him without insulting her. The comment lands, even when she is too young to name it, and it lodges somewhere she will carry for years.

"I should have never had you." — Whether spoken in anger or joke, this sentence is nuclear. Some wounds cannot be retrieved. This is one of them. If it has ever come out of your mouth, go to her. Apologize. Tell her it was a lie, that you do not mean it, that you were wrong. Pray that God fills the crater it made.

"You're too sensitive." — She is not too sensitive. She is feeling what she is feeling, and you are telling her the feeling is invalid. A child who hears this repeatedly learns to distrust her own emotional responses — and will spend her adult life struggling to believe what her own gut tells her.

"Because I said so." — It is tempting. It is efficient. It also teaches her that authority does not require reasoning. That the answer to "why" is the raw fact of who is bigger. For serious discipline, state the principle underneath the rule. "Because this is unsafe." "Because this dishonors God." "Because this hurts your sister." Reasoning teaches. "Because I said so" only enforces.

"Don't be a baby." — When he is hurt. When he is scared. When he is crying. That sentence teaches him to hide his feelings from you — and from himself. A child who learns that grief is a weakness becomes an adult who cannot process it. You do not want to raise that adult.

"Why can't you be more like your sister?" — Never. Compare them only to themselves. Never to each other. The moment you begin ranking your children against one another, you have fractured their relationship with each other and with you. Some sibling wounds are lifelong. Most of them started with this sentence.

"You're lazy. You're stupid. You're ugly." — Identity labels leveled at a child become the sentences she repeats in her own head decades later. Your mouth is shaping her interior monologue. Speak accordingly. You can address the behavior without branding the person.

"If you don't stop, I'm going to leave you here." — Do not threaten abandonment. Children believe what their mothers say. The threat to leave — even when you never would — creates a foundational anxiety about whether you can be trusted. Discipline without this tool. It is more damaging than you think.

"I'm disappointed in you." — Be careful with this. There is a time and place — occasionally — for the sentence. But it lands heavily, and it can land repeatedly until she is constructing her adulthood around the fear of disappointing you. Use sparingly. Pair with reconciliation.

"I wish you were..." — Taller. Thinner. Smarter. Quieter. Less sensitive. More athletic. More like your brother. Less like your uncle. Anything but what she is. The child who hears "I wish you were..." has been told her actual self is inadequate. That is a wound that takes decades to heal. Do not open it.

List 7: Ten Ways to Discipline Without Crushing Their Spirit

Stay calm before you engage. — Discipline delivered in rage is not discipline. It is venting. If you cannot address the infraction without losing your temper, take five minutes. Step outside. Pray. Then come back. The delay does not weaken the correction — it strengthens it.

Address the behavior, not the child. — "That was a lie" is correction. "You are a liar" is a label. The first is a behavior she can change. The second is an identity she will internalize. Keep the correction about what she did, never about who she is.

Be consistent. — The rule that is enforced on Monday but not Tuesday is not a rule — it is a mood. Children need the rules to be predictable. They also need the consequences to be predictable. Inconsistency produces anxious, manipulative children — not because they are bad, but because they are trying to read the weather.

Let the consequence match the infraction. — The small thing does not earn the big consequence. The big thing does not earn the small one. When the punishment is disproportionate, you are not teaching her about responsibility — you are teaching her about the arbitrariness of power. Calibrate.

Explain the principle underneath the rule. — "We do not speak to each other that way because our words are supposed to build each other up." "We share because we are a family, and the family takes care of each other." The rule without the principle is arbitrary. The principle with the rule is formative.

Discipline in private. — Do not correct her in front of her friends, her siblings, her grandparents, the other soccer moms. Take her aside. Speak to her. Restore her. A child corrected privately retains her dignity and receives the correction. A child corrected publicly has just learned that humiliation is part of how her mother loves her.

Affirm after you correct. — The correction is not the end of the interaction. The embrace is. Hug her. Tell her you love her. Tell her you are proud of her for receiving the correction. Close the loop. A child who is disciplined without the closing embrace carries the correction as rejection.

Be willing to adjust. — If the discipline you are using is not working, change it. Not because you are giving in, but because you are parenting the child in front of you — not a theoretical child. Different children need different approaches. The mother who is rigid about her discipline philosophy is the mother who is not actually paying attention to her child.

Discipline from love, not from fear of how she will turn out. — Discipline anchored in love will form her. Discipline anchored in fear will terrify you both. You cannot control every outcome. You can shape the values. Trust the process. Release the outcome to God.

Apologize when you discipline wrongly. — You will. You will be too harsh one day, too lenient the next. You will punish the wrong child, or punish for the wrong reason. When you realize it, apologize. "I was wrong to do that. I'm sorry." That sentence does not weaken your authority. It establishes your trustworthiness.

List 8: Ten Ways to Pass Down a Living Faith

Let them see you in the Word. — Your children know what you care about by what you make time for. If they never see you read scripture, they will not grow up believing scripture is for daily life. Let your Bible be visible. Let them see the notes in the margin. Let them hear you say, "I was reading this morning, and this stood out to me..." Faith that is performed only on Sundays will be inherited only as performance.

Pray out loud, in front of them, about normal things. — Before the meal. Before the car ride. Before the test. When you cannot find your keys. When the doctor called. Let them see that prayer is not reserved for emergencies or for church. It is the air their mother breathes. That image becomes the template for how they will pray twenty years from now.

Answer their hard questions honestly. — When she asks why Grandma died. Why there are wars. Why God allows the thing she cannot understand. Do not give her a sanitized answer. Do not pretend the questions are not real. Sit in the hard question with her. Offer what the scripture says. Acknowledge what you do not understand. A child whose hard questions are received honestly is a child who can bring her harder questions, twenty years later, to the same faith.

Do not protect her from every church imperfection. — She will see people fail. A pastor who fell. A church that split. A Christian who behaved badly. Do not explain it away. Do not pretend it did not happen. Let her see that the church is full of sinners, that God uses flawed people, and that our faith is not dependent on the perfection of any human. A faith that can survive church disappointment is a durable faith.

Teach her the stories before you teach her the rules. — The Bible is a story before it is a rulebook. Tell her about Joseph and his coat. About Ruth and Boaz. About David and Goliath. About Esther. About Mary. Let her meet the characters before you lecture her on the principles. The stories will do the teaching at a level no lecture can reach.

Celebrate the Christian calendar. — Advent. Lent. Easter. The ordinary seasons. Mark them in your home. Not because the rituals save anyone, but because they build a rhythm that anchors the year. A home with a Christian calendar is a home where the faith is not a Sunday appendix to life. It is the shape of the year itself.

Serve together as a family. — Bring her to the food bank. To the nursing home. To the neighbor who needs help. Let her see her faith moving from the living room into the world. Service is faith in motion — and a child who serves with her family grows into an adult for whom service is automatic.

Let her pray when she cannot sleep. — When she is scared. When she is worried. When the thing at school is overwhelming. Lay your hand on her and pray. Teach her to pray herself. The child who has been prayed over on her pillow is a child who will pray over her own pillow long after you are gone.

Do not fake it. — Children have a radar for performance. If your faith is a show, they will see it — and they will leave it as soon as they are old enough to. Let them see your real faith. Let them see you doubt, struggle, and return. Let them see your prayer for your own healing. Your honesty about your own faith is the most compelling argument for it.

Hand the faith over and let it be theirs. — As she grows, her faith will look different than yours. Different expressions. Different emphases. Different church traditions. Maybe even different denominations. Do not mistake that for apostasy. Your job was not to replicate yourself. Your job was to hand her to the God who can hold her. Release her into His hands. He is more faithful than you are.

List 9: Ten Ways to Mother When You're Running on Empty

Admit that you are empty. — Out loud. To your husband. To your closest friend. To God. The mother who pretends she has gas in the tank when she doesn't is the mother who will crash into her children. Honesty about depletion is the first act of repair.

Lower the bar on the non-essentials. — Cereal for dinner. Unfolded laundry. The house a wreck. In a depleted season, the essentials are: food in their stomachs, love in their ears, and their mother functional enough to be present. Everything else is optional. Let it be optional.

Ask for help — specifically. — Not "I'm struggling, can someone help." That vague cry is hard to answer. Say: "Can you take the kids Saturday morning?" "Can you pick up groceries Tuesday?" "Can you come sit with me for an hour so I can cry?" People want to help. Give them something they can actually do.

Protect the minimum rhythm. — Even in a depleted season, protect a few foundational rhythms. One walk outside a day. Fifteen minutes in scripture. A shower. One conversation with your husband. These small rhythms will keep you from drowning. Let everything else slip. Protect these.

Stop pretending you're fine. — To your husband. To your mother. To your pediatrician. To the women at church. The mother who pretends she is fine while drowning is the mother who gets overlooked — because no one can see what she refuses to show. Tell the truth. The help will come when the truth is spoken.

Delegate one thing, permanently, that is draining you. — Not for this week. For the foreseeable future. The meal you could order instead of cook. The cleaning you could hire. The yard you could outsource. The volunteer role you could quit. Find one thing and let it go. Permanently. Create margin.

Rest without guilt. — The nap. The bath. The two hours alone with a book. These are not indulgences. They are necessities. The mother who rests is the mother who can mother. The mother who runs on fumes is the mother whose children are absorbing her exhaustion like a contagion.

Cry when you need to. — Not in front of them, if you can help it. But cry. Alone in the car. In the shower. In your closet. Tears are not a failure of mothering. They are a release valve. The mother who refuses to cry is the mother who will eventually explode — or implode. Release the pressure.

Take the season seriously — but not personally. — The depleted season is a season. It is not the whole story. It is not evidence that you are a bad mother. It is evidence that you are a finite human being doing one of the hardest jobs a human can do. Recognize the season for what it is — and refuse to make it a referendum on your worth.

Go to God in your emptiness — not in spite of it. — Do not wait until you have cleaned up, gotten it together, or earned your way to prayer. Go to Him exhausted. He will not be surprised. He has seen this before. The God who met Hagar in the wilderness meets depleted mothers in the middle of their worst week. Bring Him the empty tank. He has always been able to fill it.

List 10: Ten Ways to Release Them Well

Start preparing yourself long before the day. — The release begins when they are two, not when they are eighteen. Every stage is practice. Preschool is a small release. Summer camp is a bigger one. The first sleepover. The first drive alone. Practice releasing them in small doses so the big release does not undo you.

Do not build your identity on their presence. — If the only thing you are is a mother, the empty nest will ruin you. You are a woman — a whole woman, with gifts and friendships and a faith and interests and a marriage to tend. Cultivate all of it, throughout the years of active mothering. The woman who has developed her full self is the woman who releases her children with grace — and then steps into the next chapter of her life without collapse.

Let them make their own choices. — About college. About career. About marriage. About faith expression. About where to live. Your opinion matters — but it is not binding. The mother who tries to control her adult children's decisions loses her adult children. The mother who releases her children to their own wisdom keeps a seat at their table for the rest of their lives.

Do not compete with the spouse they marry. — Their loyalty is supposed to shift. "For this reason a man will leave his father and mother and be united to his wife." This is not betrayal — this is design. The mother who does not understand this will wage a quiet war with her daughter-in-law or son-in-law for the rest of her life. The mother who does understand it welcomes the new spouse and steps into the grandmother seat with grace.

Give your opinion only when asked. — They will make decisions you would not make. That is not evidence of rebellion. That is evidence of adulthood. Keep your mouth closed. Wait to be asked. When asked, answer honestly — once, briefly, without a lecture. Then close the topic. The mother who gives unsolicited advice is the mother whose advice stops being solicited.

Let them fail without rushing to rescue. — They will make choices that hurt them. They will struggle with money, with jobs, with relationships. Do not rescue every failure. The growth is in the failure. The mother who keeps bailing her children out of the natural consequences of their choices is the mother who keeps them children long after they should be adults.

Keep praying — but stop controlling. — The shift from mothering to grandmothering is a shift from doing to praying. You will pray for them more in the second half of your life than you did in the first. That is not resignation. That is the most powerful tool you have ever had. Prayer reaches where your hands cannot.

Do not guilt them into visiting. — The mother who makes her adult children pay an emotional tax for every visit is the mother whose children begin to dread the visit. Make your home the place they want to come. Welcome them without keeping score. The visits multiply when the guilt disappears.

Welcome the grandchildren without hijacking the parenting. — Your daughter-in-law's parenting will not be your parenting. Bite your tongue. Follow her rules in her house. Support her decisions in front of the children. Be the grandmother who is invited back — not the one tolerated because the kids love her.

Bless them aloud — into the next chapter. — At the wedding. At the graduation. At the sending. Say the blessing out loud. Pray over them. Tell them what you believe God has called them to. Speak the future over them. The mother's blessing is one of the most powerful sentences in scripture, and you get to speak it. Do not stay silent at the pulpit moments.

MOTHERHOOD: QUOTES

"Behold, children are a heritage from the Lord, the fruit of the womb a reward." — *Psalm 127:3*

"Train up a child in the way he should go; even when he is old he will not depart from it." — *Proverbs 22:6*

"God gave me my family and He gave me my career." — *Ainsley Earhardt, The Light Within Me*

"Her children rise up and call her blessed; her husband also, and he praises her." — *Proverbs 31:28*

"Women of the Bible were not secondary characters, but central figures in God's story." — Adapted from Shannon Bream, The Mothers and Daughters of the Bible Speak

"These words that I command you today shall be on your heart. You shall teach them diligently to your children." — Adapted from Deuteronomy 6:6-7

"Gratitude is a lifestyle. A hard-fought, grace-infused, biblical lifestyle." — Nancy DeMoss Wolgemuth, Choosing Gratitude

"Can a woman forget her nursing child, that she should have no compassion on the son of her womb?" — Isaiah 49:15

"Just because we are waiting, does not mean that God isn't working." — Sadie Robertson Huff, Live on Purpose

"No, as hard as this is, my baby is a blessing, not a burden." — Allie Beth Stuckey, You're Not Enough (and That's Ok)

MOTHERHOOD: PUTTING IT INTO PRACTICE

Tonight, tell each of your children one specific thing you love about who they are becoming. — Not what they did. Who they are. Watch their faces. Repeat next week.

Apologize to one of your children this week for a specific thing. — Be concrete. "When I said that to you on Tuesday, I was wrong. I'm sorry. Forgive me." Model repair.

Pray out loud over each child this week. — Hand on their shoulder. Name them by name. Ask God for specific things for their life. Let them hear you interceding.

Remove one screen-based thing from the rhythm of your home for thirty days. — Not as punishment. As experiment. See what fills the space.

Have one meal a week with no phones at the table for anyone. — Parents included. Start with one. Watch the conversation change.

Write each of your children a short letter this month. — By hand. Not for a special occasion. Just because. Tell them what you see in them. Put it in an envelope. Let them keep it.

Identify one thing you are doing as a mother out of guilt rather than calling — and stop. — The activity you hate but feel obligated to. The schedule you're maintaining because the other mothers are. Cut it. See what breathes.

Ask your oldest child, if they are old enough: "Is there anything I've done as a mom that has hurt you that we should talk about?" — Listen without defending. Repair what needs repair. That conversation alone can change a generation.

Put a Bible on your kitchen counter and open it at breakfast this week. — Not a lecture. Not a devotion for them. Just your own reading, visible, with you. Let them see it.

Thank God tonight, by name, for each of your children — specifically, for who they are. — Not for the idea of having children. For the specific child. Let the gratitude reshape how you see them tomorrow morning.

CATEGORY FOUR

Marriage & Devotion

List 1: Ten Marks of a Marriage Built to Last

They face each other — not parallel in front of the screen. — The marriage that endures is the marriage in which the husband and wife regularly sit across from each other, eyes on each other, phones down, and actually talk. It is the simplest thing in the world, and the rarest. The marriage in which two people live parallel lives — each glowing in front of a separate device at the end of every evening — is slowly starving, and neither of them is noticing. Face each other. Put the screens down. Do this until you die.

They forgive daily. — Not because they are saints. Because they have understood that the alternative is a marriage where every offense is kept in a ledger, and eventually the ledger becomes the marriage. The marriage that lasts is the marriage in which both people have decided that unforgiveness is a luxury they cannot afford. Offenses happen every day. Forgiveness, given every day, keeps the ledger from ever being written.

They fight well. — Not quietly. Not politely. Well. They fight about the actual issue, not the surface issue. They fight without weaponizing the children. They fight without threatening divorce. They fight without leaving for three days and coming back pretending it never happened. And they fight with an end in mind — reconciliation, not victory. The marriage that lasts is not the one that avoids conflict. It is the one that handles conflict honorably.

They have a shared north star. — A faith. A vision for their family. A sense of where they are headed together. Marriages without a shared north star are marriages in which two people are rowing in slightly different directions — and over the course of thirty years, that slight variance becomes an ocean between them. The couples who last have something above themselves that they are both serving.

They prioritize each other over the children. — This is countercultural in a parenting-obsessed age. But the children are not the foundation of the marriage. The marriage is the foundation the children are standing on. Couples who make the kids the center of everything for eighteen years often look at each other the day the last one leaves and realize they no longer know each other. Do not let that happen. The marriage comes first. The children are served by that.

They have friends who honor the marriage. — Not the single friends who treat marriage as optional, or the married friends whose own marriages are sick. The friends who build each other up. Who hold both of you accountable. Who will tell your husband he is out of line, and who will tell you the same. The couples who last have a community that is invested in the success of the marriage itself, not just in the individuals.

They touch — every day. — A hug in the kitchen. A hand on the back as one of you walks past. A kiss before the day starts. Physical touch between spouses is not only about sex. It is a language — and couples who stop speaking it begin speaking something else, usually loneliness. Touch daily. Not as a gesture. As a discipline.

They keep short accounts. — When something is wrong, they address it — within a day or two, not a month or a year. The marriage that lasts does not accumulate unaddressed grievances. By Saturday, whatever happened on Tuesday has been dealt with. Short accounts keep the relationship clean. Long accounts poison it silently.

They laugh. — The marriages that last are the marriages that still make each other laugh. Not the stand-up comedy kind. The inside joke. The glance across the room that means something only to the two of you. The humor built out of two decades of shared life. If your marriage has lost its humor, that is a warning signal, not a neutral fact. Get it back. Laughter is the oxygen of a long marriage.

They have both decided to stay — regardless. — Before the hard seasons come. Before the illness. Before the layoff. Before the child who breaks both their hearts. Before the year that almost broke the marriage. They have decided, in advance, that divorce is not on the table. That does not mean the marriage cannot be ended by unrepentant abuse or persistent betrayal — it means that both of them have agreed that quitting because it is hard is not an option. The marriages that last are the ones where both people took the option of leaving off the table long before it was tempting to reach for it.

List 2: Ten Lies the Culture Tells Wives

"You should not have to compromise." — Every marriage requires compromise. Every relationship of two full human beings requires it. The culture that tells you that compromise is a failure of your identity has never been in a real marriage. Compromise is not losing yourself. It is loving someone enough to make room for him in your life. You are not shrinking when you adjust. You are joining.

"If it gets hard, it's not meant to be." — Every marriage gets hard. The hardness is not the sign that it was a mistake. The hardness is the test that forms the marriage. The couples who last are the ones who walked through the hard seasons without bailing. The ones who say "I'm just not happy" and leave have often walked away from the exact season in which the marriage was being deepened.

"He should complete you." — He cannot. He is not equipped to. Only God is. A wife who approaches her husband expecting him to fill the God-sized hole in her will exhaust him and be disappointed in him her entire life. Release him from that role. Run to God for the completion he cannot provide. Your husband was given to you as a companion, not a savior.

"Date nights, weekly, are a luxury." — They are not. They are maintenance. The marriage that does not invest in ordinary rhythms of connection does not survive the extraordinary seasons that come at it. Weekly date nights are not optional. They are the minimum. Cut something else. Protect this.

"Sex is less important in a long marriage." — It is not. It is more important. Sex in a long marriage is the binding agent of a thousand ordinary moments. It is one of the few places in your life where you are fully known, fully present, and fully loved. A marriage that lets sex die is a marriage that is letting intimacy die — and intimacy dying in marriage is a slow leak that eventually sinks the whole ship.

"Your husband should be your best friend — and your only one." — He should not be your only one. The weight of being your sole emotional support, your only confidant, your best friend, your lover, your partner, your everything — no husband can carry that indefinitely. You need female friendships. He needs male friendships. The marriage is protected when both of you have community. The marriage is strangled when you demand he be all things.

"Marriage is 50/50." — It is not. There will be seasons where you are carrying 70%. Seasons where he is. Seasons where he is down to 20% because he is sick, or grieving, or in the valley. A 50/50 marriage is a transactional one — you are owed half, no more. The marriages that last are 100/100 — both of you pouring out, both of you trusting that it will be reciprocated across decades.

"You should never go to bed angry." — This verse is often weaponized into a rule that prolongs every argument until two in the morning, both of you exhausted and less capable of resolution than you were five hours ago. Sometimes it is wiser to sleep, pray, and address it in the morning with clearer minds. The point of the verse is that you do not let the sun set and then sunsets pile up — not that you have to resolve every fight before midnight.

"If he really loved you, he'd just know what you need." — He doesn't. He can't. Expecting your husband to read your mind is setting up both of you to fail. Tell him what you need. Specifically. Repeatedly. Without sarcasm. He is not failing you when he doesn't intuit — he is failing only when you have told him, clearly, and he still doesn't respond. Most of the "he should know" resentment is a communication problem, not a love problem.

"A strong woman doesn't need her husband." — She doesn't need him to survive. She might have survived without him. But she has chosen him, and she has chosen to build a life with him, and that means she has also chosen to let herself need him in the ways she has invited him to be needed.

Strength is not the absence of interdependence. It is the ability to be vulnerable with the person you have chosen, without losing yourself.

List 3: Ten Things Every Wife Should Know About Her Husband

He is more fragile than he looks. — Beneath the stoic exterior, beneath the jokes, beneath the "I'm fine" — there is a man who is often carrying more than he shows you. The pressures at work. The worry about the kids. The fear of failing you. The loneliness he won't name. Know this about him. Do not confuse his silence for absence of feeling. Ask gently. Create safety. He will tell you more than you think he will, if you wait.

He needs respect more than he needs romance. — Research has confirmed what scripture has said for thousands of years. Your husband's deepest marital need is to feel respected — by you, in front of others, in his own home. A wife who respects her husband publicly and privately has given him a foundation most men never receive. A wife who withholds respect — even casually, in jokes, in eye rolls — is slowly eroding something he cannot easily rebuild.

He wants to provide — even when you are also providing. — This is not about income. It is about the ancient, scripture-rooted impulse in most men to protect and provide for the woman he loves. Honor it. Whether or not you earn more than he does, let him feel that he is providing for you in the ways he is gifted to. Your respect for that impulse is part of how you nourish his manhood.

He is not a woman, and does not process like one. — He will solve when you want him to listen. He will go quiet when you want him to talk. He will need space when you need connection. These are not character flaws. They are often differences that can be navigated if you understand them. Do not keep expecting him to be a woman. Love the man you married.

He compares himself — quietly, constantly. — To other men. Other husbands. Other fathers. Other providers. He may never tell you. But he is measuring himself against the standards he has internalized, and when he falls short, he feels it. Speak to his strengths. Name the things he does well. Let him overhear you praising him to someone else. That affirmation reaches deeper than you know.

Sex is one of the ways he communicates love. — He may not say "I love you" as often as you would like. But he may be saying it, in his native language, through physical intimacy. Do not dismiss that language as less valuable than yours. Learn to speak it. The wife who honors her husband's sexuality as a legitimate expression of connection builds a marriage very few people ever build.

He remembers your criticisms longer than you think. — The offhand comment you made in the car. The joke at his expense in front of his friends. The tone you took when he tried to help with the kids. He remembers. Even when he does not mention it. Be careful. A wife's words land harder in her husband's heart than almost anyone else's.

He wants to feel wanted. — Not just accepted. Not just tolerated. Wanted. The wife who reaches for him — physically, emotionally, verbally — gives him something most men long for and rarely receive. Do not assume he knows you want him. Tell him. Show him. Do not let your pursuit of him fade.

He carries burdens he does not share with you — to protect you. — He does not want to worry you. He does not want to look weak. He does not want to add to your plate. So he swallows things that are hard for him. Create an environment in which he does not have to. "You can tell me. I can handle it." That invitation, repeated over years, will draw him out.

He needs your prayer more than your correction. — You will see his flaws more clearly than anyone else will. You will be tempted to correct, to shape, to improve him. Resist. Pray instead. The wife who prays for her husband — every day, for decades — is shaping him in ways a thousand corrections cannot. Let God do the forming. Your job is to love and to intercede.

List 4: Ten Ways to Respect Him Without Losing Yourself

Respect his role without losing your voice. — Scripture calls the husband the head of the wife — and it calls the husband to sacrificial, Christ-like love. Both are true together. You can honor his leadership in the home without becoming silent. Respect is not the same as submission-to-silence. You have a voice. Use it with honor, not against him. A wife whose voice strengthens her husband is a wife respected by any man worth his standing.

Disagree in private, honor in public. — Whatever conflicts you have, air them between the two of you — not in front of the kids, not in front of his parents, not in front of your girlfriends, not on social media. Public honor is not deception. It is discipline. It protects the marriage from outside voices that will always be willing to agree with your worst interpretation of him.

Stop correcting him in front of the children. — "That's not how we do it." "Honey, remember, we talked about this." "Dad meant to say..." These sentences, in front of the kids, are a slow drip that corrodes his standing. The children internalize that Dad is the assistant and Mom is the manager. Save the correction for when you are alone. Let him parent, in front of them, without your editorial.

Let him lead — and keep your hands off the steering wheel. — If you have asked him to take ownership of something, let him. Do not revise his plan. Do not re-do it while he sleeps. Do not complain when it does not look the way yours would have looked. The wife who cannot let her husband lead the things she has asked him to lead is the wife who is ensuring he will never lead well.

Encourage his friendships with other men. — He needs the poker night. The Saturday fishing trip. The men's group. The friendships with men who are not you. A wife who resents her husband's community is a wife who eventually becomes his only emotional outlet — and no wife was ever designed to carry all of that. Send him to his friends. Welcome them in your home. Be glad he has them.

Let him see you as a wife first, a mother second. — The children will leave. He is supposed to be the person standing next to you when they are gone. Dress for him occasionally. Make space in the bed for him. Choose him over the kids when the moment requires it. The children will benefit most, long-term, from a mother who has not abandoned her husband for them.

Speak well of him to others. — To your friends. To your family. To the pastor. To the neighbors. A wife who publicly honors her husband's character builds a reputation for him — and for the marriage — that follows both of you. A wife who constantly complains about her husband in private conversations builds the opposite. Every word is seeding something. Know what you are planting.

Believe the best about him until evidence demands otherwise. — The assumption of bad motive will poison any marriage. When something he did hurt you, start with the question: "What's the most generous interpretation of this?" Nine times out of ten, the most generous interpretation is also the true one. A wife who believes the best about her husband frees both of them from the anxious calculation of constant suspicion.

Do not compare him. — Not to your father. Not to your pastor. Not to the influencer's husband. Not to the man you dated before him. He is not them. He is your husband — and he has his own gifts, his own struggles, his own path. Comparison will make you blind to the man he actually is. Stop it the moment you catch yourself.

Disagree with conviction — but never with contempt. — You are allowed to disagree. You are allowed to argue. You are allowed to hold a hard line. What you are not allowed to do, if you want the marriage to last, is hold your husband in contempt. Contempt in marriage is the single most predictive sign of divorce. Disagree with him. Argue with him. But never look at him with contempt. If you have begun to, that is a season for confession and repair.

List 5: Ten Ways to Be a Safe Place for Him to Come Home To

Greet him at the door when you can. — Not every day. Not performatively. But when you can, stop what you are doing when he comes in, look at him, and welcome him home. The simple act of being acknowledged at the door — after a day in which no one else noticed him — is one of the most nourishing things a wife can offer. It costs nothing. It returns enormous dividends.

Ask him about his day before you launch into yours. — He will often take the first minute of the conversation and use it to decompress. Give him the space. Before you hand him the list of things that broke today, ask how his day was. Listen. Sometimes the decompression is the whole conversation. That is a gift.

Do not flood him the moment he walks in. — The child's misbehavior. The bill. The neighbor. The plumber. Let him take off his coat. Let him sit down. Give him fifteen minutes. Then engage. Every husband who has dreaded coming home has dreaded the moment of the flood. Be the wife who does not drown him the moment the door opens.

Keep the home a place of peace, not a second battlefield. — He is coming home from an environment of stress. Your home should be a contrast, not a continuation. That does not mean quiet — it means peace. Kindness. The aroma of something cooking. Laughter in the next room. A bed that smells like home. You are the architect of this atmosphere. Build it on purpose.

Let him see you glad to see him. — Not an audition of delight. Genuine, sustained gladness that he is home. Men can feel when they are welcomed and when they are tolerated. A wife who is visibly glad her husband is home communicates to him something very few people in his life ever communicate: that his presence is a gift.

Do not grill him about his friendships, his whereabouts, his choices. — Trust is the foundation of safe space. The wife who functions as an interrogator communicates that she does not trust him — and eventually, he will stop volunteering anything. Ask questions with warmth, not suspicion. Let him come to you. If there is a real concern, address it directly. But do not turn the home into a courtroom.

Let him be weak in front of you without fixing him. — When he confesses a failure. When he admits a fear. When he cries — which he will, though rarely. Do not rush to comfort him with advice. Do not give him a verse. Do not flood him with reassurance. Sit beside him. Put your hand on his arm. Let him be weak without trying to fix it. He will rise again. But only if he was allowed to sink in your presence first.

Do not hold sex over him as leverage. — Sex in marriage is not a reward for good behavior. It is not a punishment for bad. It is a bond — one of the deepest God designed into the covenant. Do not use it transactionally. A husband whose wife uses sex as leverage is a husband who will eventually stop pursuing her, because the vulnerability has become too costly.

Keep his confidences. — When he tells you the hard thing — the thing at work, the thing with his brother, the fear he has — it does not travel. Not to your sister. Not to your mother. Not to the women's small group. If he cannot trust you with his interior, he will stop showing it to you. Your mouth is part of the safe home you are building. Guard it.

Pray over him while he sleeps. — He does not have to know you are doing this. Lay your hand on his arm or chest. Pray for him by name. Pray for the burdens he did not tell you. Pray for his walk with God. Pray for his leadership of the family. A wife who prays over her sleeping husband is performing the most ancient and powerful act of love a wife can offer. And he will feel the peace of it, even when he does not know its source.

List 6: Ten Conversations to Have Before the Wedding

What do you both believe about God? — Not on the marriage questionnaire. In depth. What is your relationship with scripture? What role will faith play in the home? What church will you be part of? How will you raise children spiritually? These conversations are non-negotiable before vows. A marriage between two people with fundamentally different views of God will split on an axis neither of them expected.

What do you both believe about money? — Your savings. Your debts. Your spending habits. Your giving. Your assumptions about whose money is whose. Your attitudes about risk. Your vision for retirement. Most couples who will fight about money for forty years did not have this conversation before they married. Have it. In specifics.

What are your expectations about children? — How many. When. Who will care for them. What will discipline look like. What role extended family will play. What schools. What faith formation. You do not need to script every decision, but you need to be in the same general zip code. Differences on children can crack a marriage years after the wedding.

What do you both expect in sex? — Frequency. Openness about needs. What is and is not on the table for you. How you will talk about sex as the marriage ages. What you will do if one of you is struggling. These are awkward conversations to have — and they are infinitely more awkward to have, for the first time, during the first year of marriage. Have them now.

How do you each handle conflict? — Do you withdraw? Do you escalate? Do you go silent for days? Do you fight loudly and move on? Understanding each other's default responses before the first fight saves both of you from misinterpreting them. He is not leaving when he goes quiet. She is not hysterical when she raises her voice. Know the language.

What does extended family look like in your marriage? — How often you will see his parents. Your parents. Boundaries with siblings. How holidays will work. What role in-laws will play in your home. Couples who do not negotiate this in advance end up fighting about it for the next decade — or worse, fighting with extended family in ways that damage the marriage.

What are your career expectations of each other? — Will both of you work? Will one of you stay home? Who is willing to move for whose career? What does balance look like? What happens if one of you loses a job? What happens if one of you feels called into a lower-paying ministry? Alignment here protects the marriage from resentment in ways you will not see until you are in it.

What wounds from your past are you bringing into this marriage? — The father who left. The abuse. The prior relationship. The addiction. The depression. The things that will echo into how you love and fight and trust. Both of you are bringing things. Name them. Bring them into the light. Secrets you carry into marriage become shadows your spouse walks through for the rest of your life.

What does your ideal day, ten years from now, look like? — Not your ideal promotion. Not your ideal vacation. Your ideal ordinary Tuesday. Where are you living. Who is around the table. What is your rhythm. What matters to you about what that day contains. This question reveals alignment at a depth surface-level conversations miss.

Are you willing to commit that divorce is not an option? — Say it out loud. "I am committing to you that divorce is not on the table for me — except in the cases of unrepentant abuse or persistent betrayal. I am choosing you for life, and I am taking 'I'm not happy anymore' off the list of reasons I would leave." The marriages that last are the ones in which both people have agreed, in advance, that quitting is not a viable exit.

List 7: Ten Fights Worth Having --- and Ten Not To

Worth having: the fight about unfair division of labor. — If the household is crushing you and he is unaware, have the fight. Specifically. Without accusation. "I am drowning. I need us to redistribute." The fight is worth having because the alternative is years of resentment that will poison what he does not know he is missing.

Worth having: the fight about his absence. — If he is checked out — on his phone, at the office, in a hobby that has swallowed him — have the fight. He may not see it. The fight is the alarm. Better a loud alarm now than a silent withdrawal later.

Worth having: the fight about spiritual drift. — If he has stopped leading the family spiritually. If he has stopped going to church. If he has stopped praying with you. This is not a passive drift to accept. It is a fight to have — with love, with hope, with grace. The spiritual leadership of the home is worth contending for.

Worth having: the fight about the in-law who has crossed a line. — His mother who is undermining your parenting. Your father who is overstepping. The sibling who is disrespecting the marriage. These fights have to be had, as a couple, about what you will and will not tolerate. Avoidance here leads to years of accumulated resentment.

Worth having: the fight about money mismanagement. — The hidden debt. The secret spending. The financial pattern that is putting the family at risk. Money conversations are hard. They are also essential. Have them before the crisis, not during.

Not worth having: the fight about how he loads the dishwasher. — Let it go. He loads it differently. You load it differently. One of you has to release control. Save your energy for things that will actually matter in a decade.

Not worth having: the fight about the past offense he has already apologized for. — It is tempting to bring it back up in new fights. Resist. Forgiveness is an event. If you have forgiven him, do not resurrect what has been buried. Re-litigating the past in every new conflict will eventually make him stop apologizing for anything.

Not worth having: the fight about how his family raised him. — You are not going to fix twenty-five years of upbringing by lecturing him about it. Address specific behaviors, not his origin story. Leave his family of origin out of the fight unless it is directly at issue.

Not worth having: the fight you started because you were tired. — You know the feeling. You are exhausted, and suddenly everything he does is wrong. The socks. The chewing. The way he breathes. Name the exhaustion. Do not let it become the fight. "I am so tired, and I'm not in a good place right now. Let me sleep. We'll talk tomorrow."

Not worth having: the fight he did not actually start. — The slight you imagined. The motive you attributed. The tone you read into a neutral comment. Check yourself before you launch. Many fights that wreck marriages were fights that did not need to begin — they began because one spouse misread the other and did not pause to ask.

List 8: Ten Ways to Protect Your Marriage From the Outside World

Do not have a close male friend who is not your husband. — A work friend who is male, a professional relationship that is respectful — fine. A male friend who you text late at night, confide in about your marriage, meet for coffee alone, whose attention makes your day — no. The boundary matters. Many, many affairs have begun with "he's just a friend." Protect the marriage by not walking into that fog.

Do not complain about your husband to other men. — Not your father. Not your brother. Not your pastor, unless it is a crisis requiring intervention. Men who hear a woman complaining about her husband may — consciously or unconsciously — begin to view themselves as an alternative. Even when they do not, you have damaged your husband's standing in the eyes of another man. Complain, carefully, only to trusted female friends.

Do not let a platform become a wedge. — The time he spends on his phone. The time you spend on yours. The parasocial relationship you are both developing with people who are not each other. This is a new form of affair — not sexual, but emotional and attentional. Protect the marriage from the algorithm. Put the phones down together. Not just one of you.

Do not share the intimate details of your marriage with your in-laws. — Even if they ask. Especially if they ask. Your marriage is between you, your husband, and God. His mother does not get the details. Your mother does not get the details. Once the intimate details leave the marriage, they never fully come back. Keep them in.

Do not let your work become a marriage. — Many affairs are with coworkers. Many of them start because one spouse is finding, at work, the attention and affirmation she is not getting at home. If you feel yourself sliding toward a workplace relationship emotionally, act. Tell your husband. Tell a trusted friend. Change the dynamic at work. Do not wait until the line has been crossed.

Protect the marriage from people who do not believe in marriage. — Some voices in your life do not respect the institution of marriage. They will suggest you leave at the first hard patch. They will mock your husband. They will treat the marriage as optional. You can love these people from a distance, but you cannot give them access to your marriage. Their counsel will not serve you.

Protect the marriage from pornography. — Either of you. It is not a private hobby — it is a third party in the marriage, and it is a destructive one. Have this conversation. Set filters. Be accountable. Speak about it without shame but also without minimization. The marriages in which pornography has been given free rein are the marriages in which intimacy slowly dies.

Protect the marriage from over-scheduling. — The couple with no time together is the couple with no marriage. If your calendar has squeezed your husband out of it — between the kids' activities, the work demands, the volunteer commitments — then the calendar is winning, and the marriage is losing. Reclaim it. Cut something. Guard the time together like a sacred asset.

Protect the marriage from social media's false comparison. — The other couples who look perfect. The anniversary posts. The picture-perfect vacations. You are comparing your behind-the-scenes to their highlight reel, and you are doing it with a man who does not have the chance to compete. Stop. Your marriage does not need to be impressive. It needs to be real.

Protect the marriage with open, constant prayer — together. — The couple that prays together has a third strand in the cord, and a cord of three strands is not easily broken. Pray together. Daily. Even when it is awkward. Even when you are mad at him. Prayer as a rhythm in the marriage becomes the steel underneath every other defense.

List 9: Ten Ways to Love Him When You Don't Feel Like It

Choose him — even when the feelings are not there. — Feelings come and go. Love is a choice, often made in the absence of feeling. The woman who waits to feel like loving her husband before she does the acts of love will not stay married. The woman who chooses him, again and again, regardless of feeling, will find that the feelings eventually come back — and the marriage that was built during their absence is stronger than the one that depended on them.

Do one small act of kindness today — even if you are angry at him. — Fold his laundry. Pour his coffee. Leave a note in his bag. Small acts, done in the middle of disconnection, are a back door into reconnection. They do not require forgiveness to be complete. They just require one step, taken in faith that love is repairable.

Remember who he is at his best — not who he has been this week. — When you are in the middle of a hard stretch, it is easy to see only the flaws. Force yourself to remember. The man you fell in love with. The father at his best. The husband in the moment you were most proud of him. He is still that man — beneath whatever version of him is currently frustrating you.

Tell God about it before you tell anyone else. — Go to your prayer closet. Tell God exactly what you are feeling. The resentment. The frustration. The cold distance. Do not edit it for the Almighty. And then listen. He will often reframe what you are carrying, sometimes point out your own part in it, always remind you that he is the one who holds the marriage. Start with God. Everything else is downstream.

Do not wait for him to apologize first. — He may. He may not. You cannot control it. But the wife who is willing to go first — who offers peace, who initiates reconciliation, who reaches across the silence — is the wife whose marriage keeps getting repaired. Pride will keep you stuck. Humility gets you back to love.

Lower the threshold for what counts as "a good day." — Some weeks, a good day is just that no one yelled. That you both went to bed civilly. That he made you laugh once. Do not expect every day of a long marriage to feel like the honeymoon. The marriages that last are the ones in which both people have adjusted their expectations to match the season they are in.

Remember that he is also trying. — He may not be doing it the way you would. He may be failing more than you think he should. But most husbands are trying harder than their wives give them credit for. Assume the effort. Notice the attempt. Affirm what he is doing, even if it is imperfect. Positive reinforcement works on men. Criticism rarely does.

Look at old photos. — Pull up the wedding photos. The honeymoon. The early years. The first child. When you have been distant from him for weeks, the pictures are a reorientation. They remind you who you chose and why. Most of the time, the man in the photo is still the man in the kitchen — just with more gray hair and more baggage.

Touch him first — even when you don't feel like it. — Put your hand on his back as you walk by. Hug him without being asked. Kiss his cheek before you go to bed. Physical touch initiated in the middle of disconnection begins the reopening of a door neither of you has been walking through. The body often leads the heart back. Let it.

Tell him you love him, out loud, when the mood is wrong. — Not because you feel it in that moment. Because it is true. Saying the words in the middle of distance is a declaration — to him, to yourself, to God — that love is a commitment you have made, not a weather pattern you are tracking. And the declaration itself often begins to shift the weather.

List 10: Ten Ways to Rebuild When the Marriage Is Breaking

Tell the truth to yourselves — and to each other. — The first step in rebuilding anything is an honest assessment of what is broken. Not what you wish were broken. What actually is. Sit down. Write it out. Speak it out loud. Most marriages on the edge are on the edge because honesty was replaced by performance years ago. Start by telling the truth.

Get a counselor — not a friend pretending to be one. — A trained, pastoral or clinical counselor, with experience in marriage restoration. Not your sister. Not the pastor's wife. Someone trained. And go together — even if only one of you wants to. The marriage that uses the resource of a trained third party has a significantly higher chance of being rebuilt.

Stop looking for the door. — As long as either of you has one foot out the door, nothing can be rebuilt. Both of you have to agree, explicitly, that for the duration of the rebuilding work, the door is closed. Not locked forever — but closed for now. You cannot build while also planning an exit.

Identify the root, not just the symptoms. — The fighting, the silence, the distance — these are symptoms. The root is usually something older: unhealed wounds, chronic resentment, a breach of trust, a season of neglect. Work backward to the root. Address what is actually broken, not just the surface conflict.

Rebuild trust one specific commitment at a time. — Vague commitments do not restore trust. "I'll be better" does not restore trust. Specific, observable, measurable actions do. "I will be home by six every day for the next ninety days." "I will not touch a drink for a year." "I will show you my phone any time you ask." Specificity rebuilds. Generalities do not.

Confess your own part — before you name his. — Every failing marriage has two contributors, even when one contributor has done far more damage. The spouse who walks in saying, "Here is what I have done wrong" changes the dynamic immediately. Pride says, "He has to apologize first." Humility says, "Let me go first." Go first.

Forgive the confessed — and mean it. — If he confesses, name it, repent of it, and change — forgive. That does not mean you trust immediately. Trust is rebuilt over time through observed faithfulness. But forgiveness can happen in a day. Refusing to forgive what has been confessed and changed is an offense of its own.

Re-establish the basics. — Eat one meal a day together. Go for a walk once a week. Pray together each morning. Have sex on a schedule if you have to. These small, basic rhythms are the scaffolding on which a rebuilt marriage is reconstructed. You do not rebuild a house starting with the roof. You rebuild it starting with the floor.

Protect the marriage from the people who want it to fail. — Some people in your life do not want your marriage to survive. They have invested in your unhappiness. They will whisper that you deserve better, that he will not change, that you should leave. Identify those voices. Distance yourself from them during this season. You need voices that are cheering for the repair, not the dissolution.

Invite God into the center. — If you have not prayed together in years, start. If you have not been in scripture together, open a Bible. If you have walked away from church, go back. A marriage that is being rebuilt without God at the center is a marriage trying to do the impossible. Invite Him in. He is the one who binds what two people cannot bind themselves.

MARRIAGE & DEVOTION: QUOTES

"Therefore what God has joined together, let no one separate." — Mark 10:9

"Husbands, love your wives, as Christ loved the church and gave himself up for her." — Ephesians 5:25

"My marriage with Charlie was the best thing that ever happened to me." — Erika Kirk, Phoenix memorial, 2025

"Above all, love each other deeply, because love covers over a multitude of sins." — 1 Peter 4:8

"To trust God is to trust His timing." — Lysa TerKeurst, It's Not Supposed to Be This Way

"Let marriage be held in honor among all, and let the marriage bed be undefiled." — Hebrews 13:4

"One moment in the presence of God is better than a thousand moments outside of it." — Kari Jobe, CBN interview

"A cord of three strands is not quickly broken." — Ecclesiastes 4:12

"True love is giving, not getting." — Nancy DeMoss Wolgemuth, Becoming a Woman of Discretion

"I'll follow where You lead." — Tasha Cobbs Leonard, Do It Anyway Devotional

MARRIAGE & DEVOTION: PUTTING IT INTO PRACTICE

Put a weekly date night on the calendar for the next three months. — Book a sitter. Make the reservation. Do not cancel. Protect it like a church service.

Ask your husband this week: "What's one thing I could do that would make you feel more loved?" — Listen without defending. Then try to do it — sincerely, for thirty days. Watch what shifts.

Write down three things you admire about your husband — and tell him about each one this week. — Not bundled together. One at a time. At different moments. Let him hear the specific affirmations land.

Pray for your husband every morning this week, by name, specifically. — Not a general "bless him." Ask God for specific things. His work. His spiritual life. His health. His leadership. Tell him, at the end of the week, that you prayed for him. Let him know he is being held up.

If there is a fight you have been avoiding, schedule it. — Pick a time. Pick a place. Name it for what it is: "I need us to talk about X this weekend." Go in with a goal of resolution, not victory.

If there is an offense you are still carrying from three months ago — forgive it, or address it. — Do not carry it silently any longer. Either bring it up to resolve, or release it in prayer. Do not let it continue to shape the marriage invisibly.

Touch your husband every day this week without sexual agenda. — Hand on his back. Kiss in the kitchen. Hug when he walks in. Make it a rhythm.

Identify one way you have been disrespecting him subtly — and stop. — The eye roll. The sarcastic tone. The correction in front of the kids. The joke at his expense. Name it. Stop it. Watch what happens in thirty days.

Have one conversation this week about something beyond logistics. — Not the kids' schedule. Not the bills. A real conversation. What you are thinking about. What you are afraid of. What you are hoping for. Remember that you married a person, not a co-manager.

Write your husband a letter this week — by hand — telling him why you chose him and why you would choose him again. — Put it in his bag. Let him find it during the week. A letter lasts longer than a text. He will read it more than once.

CATEGORY FIVE

Leadership

List 1: Ten Marks of a Woman Who Leads Without Apology

She leads because she was built to — not because she was given permission. — The woman who waits for permission to lead will wait forever. The culture that calls itself progressive still hesitates when a woman steps forward. The church that preaches the priesthood of all believers still sometimes forgets that half the priesthood is female. The woman who leads without apology is the one who has stopped asking and started stepping. She carries her authority the way a fish carries water — unconscious, essential, non-negotiable. The leadership was always there. She simply stopped apologizing for it.

She does not soften her competence to make men comfortable. — There is a specific, exhausting act that women have been trained to perform: the downplaying of their own qualifications so that the men in the room do not feel threatened. The self-deprecating joke about how she doesn't really know what she's doing. The question framed as a request when it was really a recommendation. The idea credited to someone else so it would actually be heard. She stops doing this. Not because she is trying to be difficult. Because she is done being small.

She leads with clarity, not with apology. — "I'm sorry, could I just say — " is not leadership. "Here is what I think we should do, and here's why" is. The woman who leads without apology has stopped prefacing every sentence with a softener and started letting her words land. She is not harsh. She is clear. And clarity, in a woman, is not aggression. It is respect — for the room, for the work, and for herself.

She takes up the space she was given. — She does not shrink in the chair. She does not squeeze to the edge of the meeting. She does not apologize for having an office, a title, a voice. The space was given to her for a reason. She occupies it fully. Shrinking is not humility. It is fear wearing humility's clothing. The woman who leads takes her seat and fills it.

She delegates without guilt. — The woman trained to do everything herself — because that was how she proved her worth for two decades — has to unlearn that instinct the moment she becomes a leader. Leaders delegate. Leaders trust other people to execute. Leaders stop trying to earn their position through effort and start earning it through vision. She hands off the task. She does not hover. She does not micromanage. She leads.

She corrects without destroying. — A woman who leads without apology is willing to say, "That is not good enough, and here is why." She does not soften the correction into uselessness. She does not harden it into cruelty. She speaks directly and respectfully, and the person hearing it walks away with a better path forward rather than a wound. This is the hardest skill in leadership, and the rarest — especially for women who have been told all their lives to be nice.

She does not apologize for her ambition. — The desire to build, to expand, to take on more, to lead bigger — this is not unfeminine. It is the image of a creative God expressed through a woman who takes her gifts seriously. The world has tried to convince women that ambition is selfishness. It is not. Ambition without integrity is selfishness. Ambition with stewardship is calling. She pursues the bigger thing — because she was made to.

She takes credit when she earned it. — She does not steal it. She does not inflate it. But when she did the work, when she led the initiative, when she was the one whose judgment carried the day — she says so. Out loud. Without apology. The woman who constantly deflects her own contribution to make others comfortable is not being humble. She is training the room to forget who actually did the work. Stop training them. Take the credit. It is yours.

She protects her team. — She takes the hit when her people get blamed for something she authorized. She does not throw them under the bus to save herself. She stands in front of them — and when the storm comes, she absorbs it. That loyalty is the currency that buys her the kind of team that runs through walls for her. Leaders who sacrifice their people to protect themselves are leaders in title only.

She leads with her life, not with her title. — The title on the door is the least interesting thing about her leadership. What makes her a leader is the way she lives — the way she shows up, the way she speaks, the way she handles failure, the way she treats the person with nothing to offer her. Titles are given. Leadership is earned. And the woman who leads without apology has understood that every interaction is evidence of whether she deserves the one she holds.

List 2: Ten Things That Happen When a Woman Leads Among Men

The room recalibrates. — Whether they admit it or not, a room of men adjusts when a woman steps into the lead position. Some lean in. Some lean back. Some test. The woman who leads without flinching through the recalibration is the woman who earns the room — not by asking for it, but by being so clearly the right person that the recalibration becomes irrelevant.

Her ideas are often credited to someone else. — She says it at 10:04 a.m. A man says the same thing at 10:17 a.m. and the room responds as if he invented fire. This happens. It is a fact of gendered professional life. The woman who leads knows it will happen and prepares accordingly. She documents. She restates. She says, "As I mentioned earlier — " without shame. She does not let her ideas be quietly annexed.

She is called "aggressive" for behaviors that would be called "assertive" in a man. — The same directness. The same willingness to push back. The same clear communication. When a man does it, he is "a strong leader." When she does it, she is "difficult." She does not adjust her leadership to the double standard. She keeps leading — and she lets the label sit on the people who use it, not on her.

The men who are secure respect her immediately. — And the men who are not will test her for a while. The secure ones see her leadership and treat it as what it is — leadership. They do not feel threatened because their manhood is not built on female deference. They work with her, disagree with her, learn from her, contribute to her — as they would with any peer. The secure men become her allies. The insecure ones become her education.

She has to prove herself more than once. — She will enter rooms where her track record is dismissed and she has to establish herself again. New clients. New teams. New boards. A man's credentials travel with him. Hers often have to be re-earned. The woman who leads accepts this — not as fair, but as real — and keeps proving herself without resentment, because the alternative is to stop leading, which is not an option.

Her appearance is commented on in ways men's are not. — What she is wearing. How she styled her hair. Whether she looks tired. Whether she looks too young, too old, too put-together, too casual. She cannot win. She dresses for herself — professionally, appropriately, confidently — and she does not spend one ounce of her leadership capital worrying about appearance commentary. She has work to do.

She will sometimes be the only woman in the room. — For years. Maybe for a decade. She will sit at tables where she is the single female voice in a sea of men, and she will feel the weight of that. She carries it. Not as a burden — as an assignment. She leads well because she knows that the women watching her ascent are watching to see whether it is possible. She makes it possible by doing it.

She builds other women as she rises. — Not to create a faction. To widen the path. The woman who gets to the top and pulls the ladder up behind her has misunderstood her own position. Her leadership is not just personal — it is intergenerational. She mentors. She promotes. She recommends. She makes the table larger, not smaller. And thirty years from now, the women in her field will still be benefiting from it.

She learns to translate. — The communication styles that were built in male-dominated rooms are not the only legitimate ones, but she learns to read them. She learns when directness lands well and when it lands like an attack. She learns the rhythms of the rooms she leads in — not to assimilate, but to be effective. Effective translation is not capitulation. It is leadership.

She does not pretend to be a man — and she does not apologize for being a woman. — She leads as herself. Her instincts. Her voice. Her judgment. Her way of seeing the room. These are her assets, not her liabilities. The woman who tries to lead by mimicking male leadership is borrowing a playbook that was not written for her. The woman who leads as herself — fully, authentically, without apology — brings something the room needed and didn't know it needed.

List 3: Ten Ways to Command Respect Without Demanding It

Show up prepared. — More prepared than the men in the room. More prepared than is strictly necessary. This is not fair — but it is effective. Preparation is the foundation of respect. The woman who knows the numbers, the history, the players, and the angles is the woman whose voice carries weight — because she has earned it before she ever opens her mouth.

Speak less — and mean more. — The woman who contributes to every discussion dilutes her voice. The woman who speaks deliberately, when she has something worth saying, is the woman the room listens to. Do not fill silences for the sake of filling them. Let your words be rare enough that they are valuable.

Keep your promises. — If you said you would deliver by Friday, deliver by Friday. If you said you would follow up, follow up. The woman who keeps her word — without excuse, without explanation, without the excuse that she's busy — is the woman who has built the one thing no title can create: trust. And trust is the bedrock of respect.

Correct in private. Praise in public. — When someone you lead makes a mistake, address it privately — firmly, clearly, without humiliating them. When they succeed, celebrate them publicly — loudly, genuinely, without qualifying. The woman who operates this way creates a team that protects her reputation as fiercely as she protects theirs.

Hold your composure. — The meeting that goes sideways. The colleague who attacks. The crisis that lands in your lap. The woman who keeps her composure when the room is coming apart is the woman whose leadership is remembered. Panic is contagious. So is calm. Be the source of the calm.

Speak the truth — even when it's unpopular. — The easy thing in any room is to tell the room what it wants to hear. The woman who commands respect is the one who says the hard thing — gracefully, but directly — because the room needs to hear it. Truth-tellers are rare. The ones who do it without grandstanding are rarer still. Be that one.

Do not gossip. — The woman who participates in the whispered conversations about absent people is the woman who has just signaled that she is not safe. Anything said about someone else today will be said about the listener tomorrow. Refuse to participate. Leave the room when it starts. The silence of your refusal will do more for your respect than any speech could.

Dress like you respect yourself. — Not for anyone else. For yourself. Clothing that fits, that is professional, that communicates the role you hold — this matters. It is not superficial. It is a signal. The woman who shows up looking like she takes her position seriously has already started the conversation before she opens her mouth.

Handle disagreement without becoming personal. — "I see it differently — here's why" is not an attack. Neither is "I don't think that data supports that conclusion." The woman who can disagree without attacking the person, and who can absorb disagreement without taking it personally, is the woman who leads above the fray. That composure is magnetic.

Do the work no one else wants to do. — The unglamorous task. The early morning. The boring committee. The cleanup nobody else will touch. The woman who does the work that is beneath her title — without resentment, without complaint — earns a respect that no resume can build. Leadership is not position. Leadership is willingness.

List 4: Ten Ways Women Lead Differently --- and Why That's a Gift

She often sees the human before the metric. — The tendency — not universal, but common — for women leaders to notice the person behind the number is a strength, not a weakness. She sees the exhausted employee whose kid is sick. She notices the team member who has gone quiet. She catches the colleague whose performance is slipping because her marriage is failing. That attention is not distraction from the work. It is the intelligence the work requires.

She builds relational capital. — She invests in the relationships, not just the transactions. She remembers names. She asks about the family. She sends the note. She follows up. Over the course of a career, this builds a network that is not transactional — it is genuine. And when she needs something, or someone she leads needs something, that network opens doors that no resume could.

She communicates in more than one register. — She can be direct in a pitch, warm in a mentoring conversation, firm in a correction, and tender at a funeral — all in the same week. The range of her emotional communication is a leadership asset, not a liability. The leader who can only operate in one tone has a narrower leadership than the one who can meet every moment in its own register.

She is often better at holding tension without resolving it prematurely. — Male-coded leadership often prizes quick resolution. Female-coded leadership often tolerates ambiguity longer — waiting for clarity, letting the situation develop, holding space for conflicting truths. Both modes have their place. But in complex, human situations, the willingness to sit with tension is often the difference between a rushed decision and a wise one.

She reads the room. — Not just the words — the energy. The body language. The silences. The things that were almost said. The woman who leads with this kind of attunement catches problems before they explode and celebrates victories before they are announced. That reading of rooms is a form of intelligence that is not captured on any test — and it is decisive.

She collaborates by instinct, not by obligation. — Many women leaders reach for collaboration as a default — not because they are weak, but because they know the best outcomes come from diverse input. She pulls in voices. She solicits perspectives. She does not decide in isolation if she can avoid it. The team that is led this way is often more invested than the team that is led by decree.

She mentors younger women without being asked. — She sees the young woman starting out — the way she sees herself at that age — and she opens the door. She gives the coaching. She shares the political map. She advocates in rooms the younger woman is not yet in. This is not favoritism. It is the intergenerational work that her leadership exists to do.

She grieves her failures more — and learns from them faster. — She feels her mistakes deeply. Some see this as weakness. It is not. The leader who does not feel her mistakes becomes the leader who keeps making them. The leader who feels them — who sits with the regret, who traces the failure back to its source — becomes the leader whose judgment improves over time.

She builds loyalty without buying it. — The teams she leads tend to be loyal — not because she pays more or promises more, but because she sees them, protects them, and invests in them. Loyalty like that cannot be manufactured. It is the byproduct of leadership done right. And it is the most durable asset any leader has.

She knows that how she leads is as important as what she accomplishes. — The male model of leadership often prioritizes the win. The female model of leadership — when it is done well — holds the win alongside the method. Did she get there with her integrity intact? Did her people still respect her? Was the culture she built worth inheriting? Those questions matter to her. And they should.

List 5: Ten Ways to Mentor the Next Generation of Women

Open the door before they knock. — Do not wait for the young woman to ask you for help. Watch for the one with promise, the one who is trying, the one who would be intimidated to ask. Reach out first. "I've been watching your work. Would you like to have coffee?" Those words change lives. Speak them.

Be honest about your failures. — The younger woman does not need a polished success story. She needs the real one — the missteps, the missed opportunities, the things you would do differently. Your failures are more instructive than your victories. The mentor who only tells her highlights is not actually mentoring. She is performing.

Teach the unwritten rules. — The political map of your industry. The meetings before the meetings. The relationships that matter. The dynamics that are never said out loud. The younger woman is trying to learn this on her own — and without a mentor, she will learn it too slowly or too painfully. Teach her what you wish someone had taught you.

Advocate for her in rooms she is not in. — Mention her name. Recommend her for the opportunity. Push back when someone dismisses her. The mentor's most powerful tool is the one the mentee never sees — the vote of confidence cast in a room she was not invited to. That advocacy opens doors no interview could.

Give her real feedback — not just encouragement. — The mentor who only encourages is not mentoring. She is cheering. Real mentorship includes the hard feedback — the "I think you dropped the ball in that meeting, and here's what I would do differently." Young women need encouragement, but they also need truth. Withholding the truth is not kindness. It is abandonment in a nicer package.

Make the introductions. — Your network is her shortcut. The twenty years of relationships you have built can be compressed into a single email from you to the right person. Make the introductions generously. Open your network to the women you are mentoring. That generosity costs you nothing and changes her career.

Help her understand her value — before she negotiates. — Young women often undersell themselves — the salary ask, the title ask, the benefits ask. Before she walks into the negotiation, coach her. Tell her what she is worth in the market. Tell her what to ask for. Tell her to ask for it without apology. The wage gap is partly a mentoring gap. Close it.

Let her see your real life. — The messy parts. The marriage that is hard. The kids who are a handful. The day you cried in your car before a meeting. The mentor who is only polished is showing a model that is not achievable. The mentor who shows the real picture is showing that the life is possible — including the hard parts.

Tell her when it is time to leave you. — Good mentorship has an expiration date. At some point, the mentee outgrows the mentor — and a good mentor celebrates that, releases her, and becomes a peer. The mentor who tries to hold on past the expiration date is protecting her ego, not the mentee. Let her fly. Clap for her.

Build a circle, not a monopoly. — Your mentee needs more than one mentor. She needs a constellation — women in different industries, different life stages, different perspectives. Be one of them, not all of them. Connect her to other women who can give her what you cannot. Mentorship is not ownership.

List 6: Ten Ways to Take a Stand Without Burning the Bridge

Speak directly — but not in anger. — "I have a concern about this decision, and I want to share it" is a different sentence from "I cannot believe you are actually doing this." The first one opens a door. The second one closes it. The woman who takes stands effectively has learned to be direct without being hostile. Clarity is respected. Fury is dismissed.

Make sure you are right before you make it a hill. — Not every disagreement is a hill to die on. Not every issue is worth the political capital. The woman who takes every stand equally loud loses the ability to signal which ones actually matter. Pick your ground. When you plant your flag, plant it where it counts.

Give them the grace of understanding your position before you're asked to. — Frame your stand with the reasoning. "I oppose this because — " rather than just "I oppose this." The stand that is explained is the stand that can be engaged with. The stand that is declared without explanation often gets interpreted as personal, not principled.

Do not personalize the disagreement. — You are standing against a decision, not against the person who made it. Keep it that way. "I disagree with this decision" is professional. "I can't believe you would do this to me" is personal. The first one lets the relationship survive. The second one rarely does.

Offer an alternative. — If you are standing against something, be prepared to stand for something. The woman who only says no is easy to dismiss. The woman who says, "Not this — but here is what I would propose instead" is the woman whose stands are taken seriously. Provide the path, not just the objection.

Leave the room dignified — either way. — If your stand wins, do not gloat. If your stand loses, do not sulk. Thank the room. Accept the outcome. Move forward. The woman who takes a stand and then handles the outcome with grace is the woman whose next stand will also be taken seriously. Grace in defeat is leadership at its most adult.

Follow up privately. — After a public disagreement, a private note to the other person often does more work than the public debate. "I know we disagreed in there. I respect you, and I wanted you to know that." That kind of care protects the relationship across the disagreement — and most professional relationships survive not because people agreed but because they handled disagreement well.

Choose your forum. — Some stands belong in the meeting. Some belong in a private conversation before the meeting. Some belong in a written memo.

Some belong in a one-on-one with the decision-maker. The woman who chooses the right forum for her stand often wins the stand. The woman who takes every stand in the most public setting often loses the war even when she wins the battle.

Be willing to be outvoted. — Sometimes you take the stand, make the argument, and lose the vote. That is the cost of being in a room with other adults. Accept it. Do not undermine the decision after it is made. The woman who takes her stand and then supports the outcome she lost is the woman whose integrity is unimpeachable.

Remember: the bridge is worth more than the stand most of the time. — Unless the stand is a true line — an ethical issue, a core principle, a hill you can actually die on — the relationship usually outweighs the win. Be someone who can be disagreed with without becoming someone's enemy. That capacity is rare, and it is priceless.

List 7: Ten Ways to Lead at Home

Lead the emotional weather. — The mother's mood is often the weather in a home. She does not have to be relentlessly cheerful. But she does have the capacity — more than anyone else in the house — to set the tone. Her calm calms the room. Her anxiety electrifies it. Her joy makes space for joy. Be thoughtful about what you are broadcasting. The whole house is tuned in.

Build the rhythms that hold the family. — Dinner at the table. Prayer before bed. The Sunday afternoon walk. The Saturday morning breakfast. The rituals that seem small are the architecture of the family. The mother who builds these rhythms — and protects them — is building a home that will hold its shape under pressure. Without rhythm, families drift.

Teach by what you do, not just what you say. — Your children are not listening to your lectures. They are watching your life. How you treat the waiter. How you speak to your husband. How you respond when you lose your temper. How you apologize. How you pray. The mother who teaches with her life is teaching more than she realizes — for better or worse.

Disciple your children spiritually — even if no one else will. — The church cannot do this for you. The Christian school cannot do this for you. The youth pastor cannot do this for you. Your children's spiritual formation is your responsibility. Read the Word with them. Pray with them. Answer their hard questions. Take them seriously. The mother who outsources spiritual leadership has outsourced the most important work of her home.

Set the standard for how your home treats each other. — Kindness. Respect. Honesty. Apology. These are the house rules — and they start with you. If you tolerate cruelty between siblings, you will grow cruel siblings. If you model contempt toward your husband, your children will learn contempt. If you speak kindly and insist on kindness, you will grow children who know how to treat human beings.

Lead your husband — quietly, collaboratively, respectfully. — This is not about usurping. This is about partnership. You see things he does not see. You notice things he overlooks. You have perspective he lacks. Bring it. Not with a lecture. With a conversation. The mother who partners with her husband in leading the home builds a marriage that is stronger than either of them alone.

Protect the margins of your family. — The activities. The commitments. The obligations. The schedule that fills every corner of every day. Someone has to say no — on behalf of the family. Often, that person is the mother. Protect the margin. Say no to the things that will crowd out the things that matter. The family needs space to be a family, and you are the one most likely to preserve it.

Lead in the hard conversations. — The talk about puberty. About pornography. About peer pressure. About faith doubts. About grief. About sex. These conversations are uncomfortable. The mother who leads into them — calmly, honestly, age-appropriately — is the mother whose children will come to her when the real moments hit. Avoidance trains children not to trust you. Engagement trains them to.

Model repentance. — When you are wrong, say so. Out loud. In front of your children. "I was wrong. I'm sorry. Will you forgive me?" The mother who does this trains children to do it — and there is no skill more valuable for a human life than the ability to repent. Modeling repentance is leadership. Refusing to repent is tyranny, even in a small house.

Know that this is the most important leadership you will ever do. — The boardroom will move on without you. The office will hire your replacement. The church will find another leader. Your children will not have another mother. The leadership you do at home is the leadership that will outlive everything else you build. Give it everything. No title you hold is more consequential than this one.

List 8: Ten Ways to Lead in Church

Lead by showing up. — Not for the program. For the people. The woman who is present — who arrives early, who stays late, who knows the names of the people three rows back — is the woman whose leadership grows naturally. Church leadership is less about title and more about presence. Show up, and keep showing up.

Teach the Word — to the women God has placed near you. — Whether or not your church has a formal women's ministry, there are women in your life who need to be discipled. Teach them. Open the Word with them. Walk them through the passages they are stuck on. The mother-daughters-in-the-faith model has existed as long as the church. Step into it.

Serve in the places no one sees. — The nursery. The setup crew. The meal trains. The visitation ministry. The woman who is willing to serve where there is no applause is the woman whose leadership is genuine. Platform-seeking in church leadership is the death of it. Shadow service is the soul of it.

Submit to the leadership of your church — respectfully, even when you disagree. — This is hard, especially in church traditions where women are under-utilized or under-respected. But the alternative — constant friction, open rebellion, chronic critique — is worse. Raise concerns through proper channels. Speak with the elders. And if the church is deeply dysfunctional, leave with dignity. But do not stay and destroy.

Raise up other women. — The older women teaching the younger. This is biblical, and it is largely absent from modern church life. Step into it. Invite younger women into your home. Open your life to them. Walk them through marriage, motherhood, loss, and faith. The church is weaker when women do not disciple other women. Help fix that.

Use your voice where you have it. — In the prayer meeting. In the small group. In the women's Bible study. In the ministry team meeting. The church often under-utilizes the voices of its women. If you have been given a voice — in whatever arena your church provides — use it. Say what the Spirit has given you to say. Do not withhold wisdom because the room is not fully ready for it.

Refuse to gossip — especially in church circles. — Church gossip is some of the most destructive gossip there is, because it wears the clothing of concern and prayer request. Do not participate. Do not pass it on. The woman who will not gossip in church is the woman who becomes a trusted confidante — because people know their secrets are safe with her.

Mother the flock that was given you. — If you have children, disciple them. If you teach, disciple your students. If you lead a Bible study, disciple the women in it. If you are a deacon, serve the people under your care. The model is always motherhood — attentive, self-giving, long-suffering, patient. The woman who leads in church with a mother's heart leads well.

Protect the vulnerable. — The women being abused at home. The children in danger. The new believers being taken advantage of. The elderly being neglected. The woman who leads in church is often the one best positioned to notice — and she must act. Call the professional. Report the abuse. Intervene. The church's witness depends on whether it protects its most vulnerable, and women are often the ones who can see when it isn't.

Point always to Christ — never to yourself. — If your leadership in church ever becomes about your platform, your reputation, your brand — stop. Repent. Recalibrate. The woman who leads in church is leading people to Jesus, not to herself. Anything else is idolatry. The best church leaders are the ones nobody particularly notices — because the ones they are leading are too busy looking at Christ.

List 9: Ten Ways to Lead When No One Is Watching

Be the same person alone as you are in public. — The leader whose private life is wildly different from her public life is living a double life, and double lives always collapse. The woman who leads when no one is watching is the woman whose integrity is seamless — the same on Tuesday morning in her kitchen as on Sunday morning at the front of the room.

Do the right thing when the cost is real. — Anyone can do the right thing when it is cheap. The test is the moment when doing the right thing will cost you — money, a relationship, a reputation, a contract. That moment, unwitnessed by any crowd, is the moment that forms your character. Leaders are made in those moments, not in front of cameras.

Keep your commitments even when forgetting would be easy. — The text you said you'd send. The favor you said you'd do. The commitment you made three weeks ago that no one is following up on. The woman who remembers — and follows through — is the woman whose yes still means yes. Small commitments, kept faithfully, are the foundation of large trust.

Pray when no one is going to know you prayed. — The hidden prayer life is the foundation of every public ministry. The woman who prays only when someone is looking has no actual connection to God. She has a performance. The woman who prays in her closet, for her family, for the people no one knows she is carrying, is the woman whose public life rests on something real.

Work hard on the days the output is invisible. — The slow Tuesday. The research phase. The season of preparation. The quiet months before anything visible happens. The woman who works faithfully through the invisible seasons is the woman whose visible seasons are fruitful — because the work was already done before the audience arrived.

Guard your eyes and your mind. — What you consume when no one is watching is forming you. The shows. The content. The books. The accounts. The woman who leads with integrity pays attention to her inputs — not because she is legalistic, but because she knows that what goes in shapes what comes out. Guard the inputs. The outputs depend on it.

Repent privately. — When you notice sin in yourself — the jealousy, the pride, the resentment, the pattern — do the hidden work. Confess it to God. Repent of it. Seek accountability if needed. Do not wait for it to become public to take it seriously. The leader whose hidden life is cleaned regularly is the leader whose public life does not have to be cleaned up later.

Keep your word to your children. — They notice the small things. The promise you made about the ice cream. The game you said you would play. The phone call you said you would make. Your reputation with your children is not built on the big things. It is built on the accumulation of small promises, kept faithfully over years. Keep them. Their trust in every authority figure they will ever meet is being calibrated through you.

Do the hidden service. — The meal taken to a family in crisis that you never mention. The note written to an old friend. The anonymous donation. The prayer prayed for the neighbor down the street. The woman who does the hidden service — where there is no credit, no applause, no visibility — is doing the kind of work that the Father sees, and He rewards.

Remember: there is no such thing as "no one watching." — The children see. The spouse sees. You see. And God always sees. The leader who lives as if she is always in His presence — because she is — is the leader whose public and private life are one unbroken witness. That is integrity. Everything else is theater.

List 10: Ten Truths About What a Woman's Leadership Leaves Behind

The daughters who saw you lead believed they could, too. — The single most powerful thing your leadership does — more than any project, any promotion, any title — is normalize it for the next generation. The girl who watched you lead does not have to ask whether a woman can. She saw it. Your leadership, for her, is proof of concept. That is legacy.

The men who worked for you or alongside you learned something about women. — Good. They needed to. Some of them had never had a female boss, or a female peer they respected, or a female leader they had to follow. You were part of their education. Your competence, your judgment, your character — all of it taught them something about women that they may not have learned otherwise. That is a gift to every woman who comes after you.

The culture you built will outlast you. — The way you treated your team. The standards you held. The tone you set. These things become the DNA of the organization or family or community — and they persist long after you are gone. Leaders who build cultures of respect, honesty, and excellence are leaving behind something durable. Leaders who build cultures of fear and manipulation leave behind rot.

The people you mentored are now mentoring others. — The women you took under your wing are now taking younger women under theirs. The generational chain you started is growing downstream from you — and in twenty years, there will be women leading well in rooms you never entered, because you taught the woman who taught the woman who taught them. That is the quiet math of faithful mentorship.

The standards you refused to lower became possible for others. — The meetings you would not hold in a hotel bar. The compromises you would not make. The integrity you would not trade. All of those refusals built a permission structure for the women after you — "if she could hold that line, so can I." Your integrity under pressure becomes their model. You were not being difficult. You were paving road.

The room you walked into changed — because you entered it. — The rooms that have never had a female voice sound different once one has been heard in them. The decisions change. The language changes. The assumptions change. Your presence, even if it felt small to you, reshaped the rooms you entered. That reshaping does not unreshape when you leave.

Your failures taught the next woman what to avoid. — Be honest about them. The mistakes you made — strategic, relational, ethical — are as instructive as your successes. The younger woman learning from you is as grateful for the failure story as for the triumph story. Do not hide the failures. Tell them. They are her shortcut to avoiding the same mistakes.

The home you led became the home your children will try to build. — For better or worse, the leadership you exhibited at home is the model your children will reach for when they are building their own homes. The rhythms. The values. The treatment of each other. The priorities. They are inheriting the template. Build one worth inheriting.

The church you served was strengthened by you — even if no one noticed. — The hours of hidden ministry. The women you discipled. The prayers you prayed. The meals you made. The children you taught. These are not footnotes. They are the infrastructure of the church. Your name may not be on a building. But the building is standing partly because of you.

Your leadership, lived out faithfully, was a sermon about God. — Everything you did as a leader preached something about the character of the God you served. Your patience. Your integrity. Your courage. Your humility. Your willingness to suffer for the right thing. The people who watched you work were, whether they knew it or not, getting a picture of Christ. Make sure the picture was accurate.

LEADERSHIP: QUOTES

"She is clothed with strength and dignity; she can laugh at the days to come." — Proverbs 31:25

"Whatever you do, work heartily, as for the Lord and not for men." — Colossians 3:23

"I've learned to do things afraid." — Christine Caine, interview with Jennie Allen

"The righteous are as bold as a lion." — Proverbs 28:1

"God is at work even amid the chaos." — Kayleigh McEnany, interview about Serenity in the Storm

"Pride goes before destruction, and a haughty spirit before a fall." — Proverbs 16:18

"Remember where your gifts come from, because it's not from you." — Carrie Underwood, American Idol, 2026

"They who wait for the Lord shall renew their strength; they shall mount up with wings like eagles." — Adapted from Isaiah 40:31

"God intended us to be joyful people." — Dana Perino, Faithwire interview

"The cries of this widow will echo around the world like a battle cry." — Erika Kirk, Phoenix memorial, 2025

LEADERSHIP: PUTTING IT INTO PRACTICE

Say one clear thing this week without softening it. — One sentence. Your actual opinion. No "just" at the front, no apology at the end. Watch how it lands. Notice whether the world ends. It won't.

Make one introduction this month on behalf of a younger woman. — Someone in your network. Someone who could open a door for her. Send the email this week. Copy her on it.

Identify one hill worth dying on — and one hill you've been dying on that wasn't worth it. — Write them down. Commit the first to memory. Release the second.

Take credit for one thing you did this week. — Out loud. In a meeting. In an email to the team. Without the deflective "we" if it was actually you. Practice the words.

Find one area where you've been waiting for permission — and stop waiting. — The project. The role. The conversation. The initiative. Permission is not coming. Proceed.

Write a note to a woman you've been mentoring — tell her specifically what you see in her. — Not general encouragement. Specific observation. What her gifts are. Where her ceiling is. What you hope for her. She will keep that note for twenty years.

Pick one thing you've been doing for image — and stop doing it. — The committee. The role. The appearance you've been maintaining. If it's rooted in performance rather than calling, release it this week.

Have one hard conversation you've been avoiding. — The employee who is not performing. The friend who has been unkind. The family member whose behavior has been crossing a line. Prepare your words. Schedule the conversation. Have it calmly.

Identify the three women who have mentored you — and thank them this month. — Write a real letter. Not a text. A letter. Tell them what they gave you. Send it. Gratitude is the currency of leadership, and you have been receiving for too long without depositing back.

Ask God this week to show you the hidden areas of your leadership that don't match the public one. — Sit with the answer. Repent of what needs repenting. Confess what needs confessing. Seek the wholeness that is the foundation of every integrity that lasts.

CATEGORY SIX

Work & Purpose

❧

List 1: Ten Ways to Know What You Were Made to Do

Notice what you cannot not do. — The thing you return to even when no one is paying you. The subject you read about for fun. The work you would do if you won the lottery tomorrow and never had to work again. That pull — the one that doesn't turn off even in the quiet — is often the fingerprint of calling. Pay attention to what doesn't let you alone.

Look at what breaks your heart. — Not in a general way. Specifically. The injustice that makes you weep. The wound you cannot walk past. The group of people you cannot stop thinking about. God often gives His daughters calling through grief — the thing that breaks her is often the thing she is meant to build something in response to. Notice what breaks you. It may be pointing somewhere.

Listen to what other people keep telling you about yourself. — "You're so good at — ." "You always know how to — ." "When I'm with you, I feel — ." The feedback you get repeatedly, from different people, across different seasons — that is often a trail of breadcrumbs leading back to your design. Other people sometimes see the gift before you do. Let them tell you.

Notice what gives you energy versus what drains you. — Not every day, because every day has drain. But in general. What is the work that, even when it's hard, fills your tank? What is the work that, even when it's going well, empties it? The shape of your energy is often the shape of your calling. The drain is not proof you should quit. But it is data worth noticing.

Consider the intersection of your strengths and the world's need. — What can you do well that the world is asking for? That intersection — where your gift meets a genuine need — is often where calling lives. Not every gift finds a match with a need the world pays for. But the question is worth asking. Your calling may live in a place you haven't looked yet.

Look at your season. — Your calling is not one thing you do for fifty years. It is a series of things shaped to the season you are in. Young single woman: one calling. New mother of three: different calling. Empty-nester: different again. The woman in a hospital bed: different still. Do not panic that your calling has shifted. Seasons change. Calling changes with them. Faithfulness to the current season is the calling of the current season.

Pray. — Ask God directly. Not once, in frustration. Regularly. "Show me what I was made for. Make it clear. Close the doors that are not mine. Open the ones that are." He answers these prayers — often not with a lightning bolt, but with a slow clarity that emerges over years. Pray it anyway. The asking is formative.

Act on what you already know. — Do not wait for perfect clarity to take the next step. Most women discover their calling in motion, not in stillness. The small yes. The first class. The initial project. The tentative side pursuit. Clarity comes through action more often than action comes from clarity. Start walking. The path reveals itself under your feet, not in advance.

Pay attention to doors that keep opening. — Some doors you have to push. Some doors swing open without pressure. The pattern of which doors open for you — the opportunities that keep finding you, the conversations that keep circling back to the same theme — is often how God directs. Not every open door is from God, but open doors, collectively, form a pattern worth reading.

Accept that your calling will feel too big — and do it anyway. — If your calling feels perfectly manageable, it is probably not your calling. The things God gives His daughters to do are usually bigger than they feel equipped for, because the doing of them is supposed to grow them. Do not wait to feel ready. You will not feel ready. Ready is not a feeling. Ready is a decision.

List 2: Ten Lies the World Tells Women About Work

"Your career is your identity." — No, it is not. Your career is what you do. Your identity is who you are. The woman who builds her identity on her career will discover — the day she is laid off, or retires, or changes seasons — that she has no self left. She traded being for doing. Your work matters. It is not the whole of you.

"If you don't 'lean in,' you're letting women down." — Every woman's calling is different. Some women are called to climb. Some are called to homemake. Some are called to nonprofit work. Some are called to plant churches. Some are called to the home for a decade and then to the marketplace. The version of feminism that tells every woman she owes the movement a climb is no better than the version of patriarchy that told every woman she owed her father obedience. Pick your own calling. Ignore the external mandates.

"Your worth is measured by your paycheck." — It is not. Some of the most important work in the world — motherhood, caregiving, ministry, volunteering, writing for the invisible audience — pays little or nothing. Some of the most lucrative work produces things the world doesn't actually need. Paycheck is one data point. It is not the measure of the woman.

"You can't have a family and a real career." — Or its inverse: "You can't stay home and still be a real woman." Both lies. Some women have families and careers — beautifully. Some women stay home and build empires inside their walls. Some alternate across decades. The picture of a flourishing woman is not one picture. It is many. Do not let anyone tell you your configuration is wrong.

"You have to hustle constantly to succeed." — Hustle culture has told a generation of women that rest is laziness and that the grind is the path. This is a lie. The women who build things that last often work hard — but they also rest hard. The unrested woman burns out. The overworked woman gets sick. The relentlessly-striving woman loses her marriage. Hustle is one tool. It is not the only tool. And for many seasons, it is the wrong tool entirely.

"You should love your job." — A job is a job. Some are pleasant. Some are grinding. Most are a mix. The expectation that you will love your work every day is a lie manufactured by people who want you to accept less in exchange for a feeling. Your work does not have to be your passion to be worth doing. Honest work, honorably done, is always a calling — even when it is boring.

"Money is the enemy." — Money is a tool. It is the love of money that is the root of evil. Money itself is neutral — it does what you point it at. The woman who handles money wisely can fund ministries, support family, give generously, and provide for her old age. The woman who refuses to engage with money will be handled by it her whole life. Learn it. Respect it. Steward it.

"Your ambition is selfish." — It depends on what the ambition is for. Ambition in service of a calling is stewardship. Ambition in service of ego is idolatry. The question is not whether to be ambitious but what the ambition is aimed at. Women have been told for too long that ambition itself is unfeminine. It is not. It is a gift — if it is aimed rightly.

"You need to work twice as hard to get half as far." — Sometimes, in some fields, this is true. Accept the unfairness and work anyway. Do not let the unfairness paralyze you. And do not use it as an excuse to underperform — because underperforming in an unfair system is still underperforming. Show up, do the work, and make the people who doubted you wonder how they missed it.

"If you haven't made it by forty, you missed it." — Sarah was ninety when Isaac was born. Moses started his real work at eighty. Anna was a widow for decades before she saw the Messiah. God's timelines do not match the world's. Some women bloom at twenty-five. Some bloom at sixty-five. Both are on time. Your work is not over at forty. For many women, it is just beginning.

List 3: Ten Ways to Carry Your Faith into Your Work

Be the most honest person in your field. — Not the one who cuts corners. Not the one who shades the truth. The one whose word is reliable — every time, even when it costs. Honesty in business has become rare enough that it is now a competitive advantage. Use it. Let your work be a place where people know they will get the truth from you, whether they like the truth or not.

Work with excellence — because He is watching. — Colossians 3:23. "Whatever you do, work at it with all your heart, as working for the Lord, not for human masters." That verse is the Christian's work theology in a sentence. You are not working for your manager. You are working for Christ. That changes everything — the quality, the attitude, the motivation. Apply it.

Treat the people under you as image-bearers. — The employees. The assistants. The vendors. The people whose names nobody higher up remembers. The Christian woman in the workplace is the one who knows every name, asks about the family, and speaks with genuine respect to everyone in the building — not because it is politically wise, but because every person is made in the image of God.

Do not participate in the gossip, the political maneuvering, the backstabbing. — The office has its games. You do not have to play. The Christian woman at work is the one who is known for not participating in the toxicity — the one people come to when they want a genuine opinion, because they know she will not weaponize their words. That reputation takes years to build and sixty seconds to lose. Guard it.

Pray over your work. — Pray before the meeting. Pray over the hard client. Pray before the interview. Pray over the project that is failing. The Christian woman's secret weapon in her work is the unseen spiritual life that undergirds everything visible. Her colleagues see the output. They do not see the prayer. But the prayer is where the strength comes from.

Do not make your job an idol. — Work matters. It does not matter more than God, your family, your soul, or your Sabbath. The woman who sacrifices everything on the altar of her career will one day discover she sacrificed the things that cannot be gotten back. Keep work in its place. It serves you. You do not serve it.

Use your influence — quietly — for the vulnerable. — The young employee being taken advantage of. The woman being passed over. The intern nobody is protecting. The customer being deceived. If you have influence, use it for the ones who don't. Jesus's heart is constantly on the vulnerable. If His heart is there, yours should be too — and at work, that often looks like being the one person who notices and speaks.

Tell the truth about your faith when it is appropriate — without weaponizing it. — You are not an evangelism machine in your workplace. You are a person who happens to follow Jesus. When it comes up, you say so — simply, honestly, without making every conversation an altar call. The witness of a faithful Christian life in a workplace often speaks louder than words. Let the life preach.

Refuse the unethical request — gracefully, but firmly. — The request that crosses a line. The thing your boss wants you to do that you cannot, in conscience, do. The compromise that would save the deal but would require lying. Refuse. Politely. Professionally. Without grandstanding. And if the refusal costs you the job — let it cost you. The Christian woman's conscience is worth more than any contract.

Trust that faithfulness will be rewarded — even if not by this employer. — You may not be promoted. You may not be celebrated. You may be passed over in favor of someone less capable and less ethical. That happens. But you are not working for this company. You are working for Him — and He sees what your manager does not. Faithfulness is always rewarded. The ledger is not always human.

List 4: Ten Things to Remember When the Workplace Wasn't Built for You

You are not imagining it. — The meetings run on a rhythm you did not set. The humor draws on references you do not share. The pathways to advancement favor patterns you don't fit. The network is not one you were included in. Some workplaces have done real work to change this. Many have not. You are not imagining the friction. It is there.

You do not have to become someone else to belong. — The temptation — to flatten your voice, mimic the style, erase the things that make you distinct — is strong. Resist it. Your difference is not a bug. It is the reason you were hired, or should have been. Translate where translation is wise. Assimilate only to the point where you can still recognize yourself.

Find your allies — and invest in them. — Not every man in your workplace is an obstacle. Many are genuine allies. Find them. Work with them. Build relationships with them. And when they advocate for you, notice it, thank them for it, and remember it. The allies matter. Do not treat every colleague as an opponent because some are.

Pick the battles that are worth it. — You will not win every fight. You will not even fight every fight. The woman who makes every slight a referendum will exhaust herself and lose credibility. Pick the battles where a principle is genuinely at stake. Let the smaller things go — not because they don't matter, but because you cannot fight them all, and the ones that matter need your full strength.

Document what happens. — When there is a pattern of bias, of exclusion, of inappropriate behavior — write it down. The date. The quote. The context. Not because you are planning to sue. Because memory gets rewritten under pressure, and you will need the record if you ever have to make a case. Protect yourself with documentation. It is not paranoid. It is professional.

Do not let the hostility make you hostile. — You are being formed by this workplace — for better or worse. If the environment is full of pettiness, do not become petty. If the culture is full of cynicism, do not become cynical. Who you are at work, over years, shapes who you are. Refuse to let a broken environment break your character.

Support the other women — even the ones who aren't your friends. — The workplace that wasn't built for women is the workplace where the women sometimes turn on each other, competing for the scraps that seem available. Do not participate. Lift the other women. Advocate for them. Share credit with them. The scarcity mentality is a lie, and the women who operate by it remain small. The ones who operate by abundance expand.

Take care of yourself more carefully than your peers take care of themselves. — The male colleagues may be running on adrenaline and takeout and ignoring their health. Do not copy them. The woman in a hostile workplace needs more rest, not less. More exercise. More Sabbath. More prayer. More therapy, if needed. The maintenance costs are higher when the environment is draining. Pay them.

Know when to leave. — Some workplaces can be changed from within. Some cannot. Know the difference. If you have given a year to an environment that is actively hostile to your presence, and nothing is moving, consider that staying may not be stewardship. It may be endurance of a situation God was asking you to exit. Prayer, counsel, and honest reflection will tell you which.

Remember: your presence matters — even if it is costing you. — The women who go next will have a slightly easier path because of what you did. That is not a small thing. That is legacy. You did not sign up to be a pioneer. You became one by showing up. And the cost of it is real, but the gift of it — to the women who follow — is real too.

List 5: Ten Signs It's Time to Stay --- or Go

Stay if you are still growing. — Not bored. Not stagnant. Still learning something, still being stretched, still gaining skills that will serve you later. Growth is the best reason to stay in a role longer than is obviously optimal. The years of skill accumulation compound later.

Go if you are dying inside every day. — There is a difference between a hard job and a soul-killing job. You can endure a hard job. You cannot endure a soul-killing job without losing yourself. If you are hollow every evening, if your family is getting the depleted version of you, if you are losing who you were — the job may be costing more than it is paying.

Stay if the calling is clear — even when the season is hard. — Callings often have hard seasons. The hard season is not, by itself, a signal to leave. If God placed you here for a reason, and the reason is still present, stay. Endure. Trust that the season is forming something. The going gets tough precisely when something valuable is being built.

Go if your integrity is being compromised. — The requests are crossing lines. The culture is requiring you to participate in things you cannot participate in. You are having to choose between keeping the job and keeping your conscience. This is not a close call. Leave. Your integrity is worth more than any job.

Stay if you are making a difference. — Even if it is slow. Even if it is unrecognized. Even if it is one person at a time. The work that matters is not always the work that pays well or is celebrated. Stay in the place where the fruit is real — even if the external metrics are underwhelming.

Go if the role is distorting your family. — The hours. The travel. The emotional load. The constant availability. If the job is eating your marriage, your children, or your health — something has to give. Sometimes the something is the job. The family is not a cost center. It is the center.

Stay if the Lord has not released you. — This one is hard to articulate but real. Sometimes you pray about leaving and the answer is simply, "Not yet." Stay where God has placed you, even when it is inconvenient, until He releases you. Moving ahead of God's release is not brave. It is reckless.

Go if the right next door has opened — clearly, and not frantically. — A door has opened. It aligns with your calling. The counsel of trusted people confirms it. The timing makes sense. Your spirit is at peace about it, not anxious. That is a door worth walking through. Do not dither. Go.

Stay if leaving would be fleeing a hard season rather than answering a clear call. — Many people mistake the urge to escape for the urge to advance. The season is hard, so they leave — only to find the next place has different hard seasons, and they left something valuable unfinished. Before you leave, ask: am I running to, or running from? The answer matters.

Go if the day you leave will be a Tuesday, and God has confirmed it. — When the departure is right, there will usually be a strange, uncharacteristic peace about it. Not excitement — peace. You will know. It may come slowly, but it will come. When you know, move. Do not linger in a role God has released you from. It is not grateful. It is small.

List 6: Ten Ways to Pursue Excellence Without Making It an Idol

Excel for God, not for applause. — The difference is internal. The work product may look similar. But the woman excelling for God is not destroyed when the applause does not come — because she was not working for the applause. She was working for an audience of One. Excellence in that mode is sustainable. Excellence for applause is a house of cards.

Accept that good enough is sometimes good enough. — Not every task deserves your maximum effort. The email to your colleague can be adequate. The casserole for the potluck can be fine. The holiday card can be unpolished. Perfectionism applied indiscriminately means you run out of capacity for the things that actually need it. Triage your excellence.

Know the difference between excellent and exhausting. — Excellent work is sustainable. Exhausting work is not. The woman who thinks she is pursuing excellence but is actually pursuing perfection is on a road that ends in collapse. Excellence has margin. Exhaustion does not. If you are always exhausted, you are probably not actually being excellent — you are being compulsive.

Rest as part of excellence, not as recovery from it. — Excellent work requires rested people. The woman who works seventy hours a week is not producing excellent work by hour sixty-five. She is producing mediocre work on caffeine. Rest is part of the work. Sabbath is part of the excellence. Do not treat rest as the reward for excellence. Treat it as its ingredient.

Pursue excellence in the small things. — The way you answer the phone. The grammar in your emails. The preparation for a meeting that feels routine. The shape of your handwritten note. Excellence in small things compounds. The woman who is excellent in small things has built the habits that produce excellence in large things.

Take pride in the work — and then release it. — When it is done, it is done. Hand it in. Send it out. Do not keep it forever, polishing it past the point of diminishing returns. The woman who cannot release her work has made the work her identity. Release it. Whether it succeeds or fails, it is no longer in your hands.

Let others critique your work without it meaning the end of the world. — Feedback is part of excellence. The woman who cannot tolerate critique has a brittle excellence — one that shatters at the first pointed comment. The woman who can receive feedback, sort the helpful from the useless, and integrate what matters has a resilient excellence. Develop that.

Notice when the pursuit of excellence has become anxiety. — Is your excellence serving you — or are you serving it? When you cannot sleep because the work is imperfect. When you cannot enjoy your family because the project is not finished. When the pursuit has become a compulsion rather than a calling. Stop. Breathe. Recalibrate. Excellence that destroys you is not excellence. It is idolatry wearing excellence's clothing.

Celebrate the excellent work of others without jealousy. — The woman whose excellence is rooted in security can celebrate other people's excellence fully. The woman whose excellence is rooted in insecurity sees every peer's success as a threat. Which one are you? If you cannot genuinely celebrate the excellence of others, something is off. Ask why.

Remember that excellence is an offering, not a trophy. — The woman who produces excellent work as an offering to God holds it lightly. She did the best she could. She gave it to Him. What happens to it next is not her concern. The woman who produces excellent work as a trophy clutches it — defends it, worries about it, cannot let it fail. One is free. The other is owned by her own work. Be free.

List 7: Ten Ways to Handle Money Wisely as a Woman

Know where it goes. — The woman who does not know where her money is going is being spent by her money. Track it. All of it. For at least three months. Categories, amounts, patterns. The awareness alone is transformative. You cannot steward what you have not measured.

Give first. — Before the bills. Before the savings. Before the latte. Give. The first ten percent — or whatever you have decided with God — goes out before anything else. This is not financial advice in the traditional sense. It is spiritual formation. The woman who gives first has ordered her life around something other than accumulation.

Build the emergency fund before the investment portfolio. — Three to six months of expenses. Liquid. Untouchable except for actual emergencies. This is the foundation of every other financial decision. Without it, one unexpected bill can destroy a carefully planned life. With it, most storms become survivable rather than catastrophic.

Do not outsource all financial knowledge to your husband. — If you are married, both of you should know what is happening financially. Both should be able to access accounts. Both should know the major decisions being made. The woman who is financially dependent without being financially informed is one terrible event away from being blindsided — and it happens more than anyone admits. Know your own finances.

Avoid the debt that enslaves. — The credit card with the balance that never goes down. The car payment that eats your paycheck. The house that is too expensive to enjoy. Debt for consumables is almost always a trap. The woman who stays out of consumer debt has freedom that the woman with payments will not understand until she escapes them.

Live below your means — deliberately. — Not because you cannot afford more. Because you are refusing to. The woman who has chosen to live at 80% of her income has built margin into her life — margin for giving, for saving, for weathering storms, for making choices that higher earners trapped in higher lifestyles cannot make. Choose the margin over the upgrade.

Invest — even if you start small. — The woman who invests consistently, over decades, even small amounts, builds wealth that the woman who waits for "when I have more" never builds. Time is the most powerful variable. Start now. Open the account. Set up the automatic contribution. Do not wait for perfect knowledge. Start imperfect.

Do not buy things to feel better. — The dopamine of the purchase lasts ninety seconds. The debt or the clutter lasts for years. The woman who buys to soothe emotions is medicating with consumerism — and it does not work. Address the feeling directly. Call the friend. Take the walk. Pray. Save the money. The purchase is the wrong answer to the right question.

Be generous without being foolish. — Give to causes that matter. Support the missionaries. Help the friend in crisis. But do not let yourself be manipulated into giving that damages your own stewardship. The line between generosity and enabling is real. Pray about it. Seek counsel. Give — but wisely.

Teach your daughters about money. — Openly. Specifically. What you earn. What you save. How you invest. How debt works. How to negotiate a salary. How to evaluate a job offer. The financial illiteracy of women across generations is not an accident — it is the result of money being kept from them. Break the pattern. Open the conversation. Give your daughters the education the culture will not.

List 8: Ten Ways to Find Purpose in Ordinary Work

Serve the person in front of you. — The customer. The client. The coworker. The patient. Every job, no matter how ordinary, involves serving another human being. The woman who does this well has found purpose — even in the smallest role. The cashier can embody the love of Christ. The receptionist can be the face of grace. The purpose is not in the title. It is in the posture.

Do the work as worship. — Wash the dishes as worship. Answer the emails as worship. Prepare the spreadsheet as worship. The category of "ordinary work" disappears when you do the work for God. What was mundane becomes meaningful. Not because the work changed, but because the audience did.

Notice the dignity in what you do. — Every legitimate job is contributing to the human community. The person who cleans the hospital is keeping patients alive. The person who answers the phone is the first voice someone hears in crisis. The person who drives the truck is the reason the store has food. Your work, whatever it is, is holding up a corner of civilization. That is not nothing.

Build relationships with the people you work with. — Even if the work is tedious. The relationships transform the experience. The coworker you pray for. The boss you genuinely respect. The employee whose life you have entered. Ordinary work with ordinary people — over years — becomes extraordinary connection. That is purpose, even if the job description does not say so.

Do your ordinary work extraordinarily well. — The bar for excellence in most workplaces is low. Meet the bar, and you are average. Clear the bar by two feet, and you are extraordinary. The ordinary job performed extraordinarily becomes a platform for influence — and often, it becomes the door to something larger.

Pray for your workplace. — The people. The leadership. The decisions being made. The customers being served. The missteps being processed. The woman who prays for her workplace carries a purpose that has nothing to do with her title. She is the intercessor. She is the priest in that office. Most of her colleagues will never know. That is fine. Jesus knows.

Stop waiting for a different job to give your life meaning. — Meaning is not waiting in a different building. The woman who thinks her purpose will begin when she gets the promotion, the new company, the next opportunity — is postponing her own life. Purpose is available in the current role. Find it. Do not outsource your meaning to a future that is not guaranteed.

Be the person the company cannot replace. — Not by being hoarding or manipulative. By being genuinely excellent, deeply relational, and quietly invaluable. The ordinary job becomes less ordinary when you become the person whose absence would be immediately felt.

Support someone else's career while you are in yours. — Your coworker who is trying to get promoted. The younger employee who is learning. The peer who is struggling. The ordinary job is full of opportunities to quietly help other people — and those opportunities give your work a dimension of purpose that the job description never mentioned.

Remember that God sees the ordinary. — He sees the hours. He sees the exhaustion. He sees the unnoticed faithfulness. The work that seems invisible is not invisible to Him. The ordinary woman doing ordinary work with extraordinary faithfulness is being watched with affection by the Father — and she is building a record in heaven that the world's metrics will never capture.

List 9: Ten Ways to Balance Ambition and Surrender

Name your ambition — honestly. — What do you actually want? The promotion. The audience. The recognition. The platform. The financial security. The body of work. Do not pretend you have no ambitions. Every adult does. The woman who names her ambitions can examine them. The woman who pretends she has none is being owned by the ones she will not acknowledge.

Submit them to God — specifically. — "God, here is what I want. I am laying it down. If You want to give it, I will receive it. If You want to redirect, I will follow. If You want to deny it, I will trust that You are good." That prayer — prayed repeatedly, with actual surrender — is how ambition and faith coexist. You do not kill the ambition. You offer it.

Pursue with effort — release with open hands. — Work hard for what you want. Train. Prepare. Apply. Network. Ask. Then release the outcome. The woman who pursues hard and releases well can handle both success and failure without losing herself. The one who pursues hard and cannot release is devastated by failure. The one who pursues softly because she does not want to want too much is wasting the ambition God gave her.

Notice when ambition becomes identity. — The moment you cannot imagine yourself without the thing you are pursuing — the title, the house, the audience — it has become an idol. Recognize it. Repent of it. Ask God to pry your fingers loose from the outcome. You can still pursue. You cannot worship.

Keep the bigger picture visible. — Why are you pursuing this? What would success here serve? What would failure here prevent? The woman whose ambitions are in service of a larger purpose — her family, her calling, her mission — has ambitions that are ordered. The woman whose ambitions exist for themselves has ambitions that have become idols. Order matters.

Be willing to be redirected. — You prayed about the promotion. It did not come. You wanted the opportunity. It went to someone else. You were sure this was the door. It closed. God sometimes redirects. Not because He does not care. Because He sees something you do not. The woman who trusts the redirection — even when it hurts — is the woman whose life is being guided by a wiser hand than her own planning.

Hold loosely the things you cannot control. — You cannot control whether you get the promotion. You can only control whether you prepared and performed well. You cannot control whether the book sells. You can only control whether you wrote it with integrity. Hold the effort. Release the outcome. This is not resignation. This is sanity.

Celebrate the wins without gripping them. — When the promotion comes, receive it gratefully. Enjoy it. Thank God for it. And then hold it loosely — because it could be taken away tomorrow. The woman who grips her wins tightly is terrified of losing them. The woman who holds them loosely is free. Win loosely.

Grieve the losses without being destroyed. — The promotion that did not come. The business that failed. The role that was given to someone else. Grieve it. Let yourself feel it. Then look up. God has not forgotten you. The story is not over. The woman who can grieve a loss without it becoming her identity is the woman whose ambition is held in the right proportion.

Remember that God's "no" is often mercy you do not yet understand. — The door that closed may have been closing a road that would have destroyed you. The opportunity that went to someone else may have been dodged on your behalf. The win that did not come may have been God's protection. The woman who trusts God in the unanswered ambitions often discovers, years later, the reason. Trust Him before you see it.

List 10: Ten Ways to Finish Your Working Years Well

Mentor the younger women. — The last decade of your career should not be about maximizing your own output. It should be about investing in the ones who will take the baton. Pour into them. Share the lessons. Open the doors. Your legacy is not the last project you delivered. It is the women whose careers you launched.

Hand off responsibilities before you have to. — The woman who clings to every role until the moment she is forced out has not finished well. The woman who begins handing off years in advance — teaching the next person, releasing the grip — finishes with dignity. Plan your transitions. Do not let them be forced on you.

Decide what your final season will be about. — Is it about finishing a body of work? Writing the book? Training the successor? Investing in community? Pivoting to a new venture? Decide. A final decade with no aim is a decade that drifts. A final decade with a clear aim is a decade that produces the capstone.

Do not try to relive your thirties. — The temptation is real — to hold onto the energy, the role, the relevance, the look. Do not. The fifties are their own country. The sixties are their own country. Each decade has its gifts. The woman who tries to stay in a previous decade misses the one she is actually in.

Care for your body in the final working decades. — You have asked a lot of it. Now ask it to carry you through the last chapters. The investments in health now — movement, sleep, nutrition, strength training — are what will allow you to finish well. The woman who neglected her body in her thirties and forties will regret it in her sixties. The one who tended it will still be hiking at seventy.

Tell people what you have learned. — Write it down. Say it out loud. Leave the record. The younger generations will not know what they do not know unless the older generations tell them. The woman who spent decades learning things the hard way has a responsibility to pass it on. Do not take the wisdom to the grave.

Repair the relationships that are still repairable. — The former colleague with whom there is still tension. The mentor whose call you never returned. The friend who drifted. The family member with whom something was left unsaid. The final years are the time to repair what can still be repaired. Make the call. Write the note. Do not leave it for later. Later has a short horizon now.

Let go of the grievances. — The colleague who undermined you twenty years ago. The boss who passed you over. The company that underpaid you. The client who stiffed you. Let them go. Carrying grievances into your final decades is the poison that corrupts an otherwise rich life. Forgiveness, finally given, is freedom, finally claimed.

Give generously — while you can still watch it work. — Do not leave all your giving to your will. Give now. Watch what your money does when it goes to the causes that matter. Watch the woman whose tuition you paid graduate. Watch the church you funded reach the community. Watch the ministry you supported grow. The gift given in person is a gift received by two.

Finish with a posture of thanksgiving. — The work was a gift. The years were a gift. The people were a gift. Even the hard seasons were shaping. The woman who finishes her working years full of gratitude — rather than regret or bitterness — is the woman whose final chapters are rich. Gratitude is the posture. Keep it until the end.

WORK & PURPOSE: QUOTES

"Whatever you do, work heartily, as for the Lord and not for men." — Colossians 3:23

"Commit to the Lord whatever you do, and he will establish your plans." — Proverbs 16:3

"God is my co-writer and my co-pilot." — Dolly Parton, interview with The Christophers

"Whatever your hand finds to do, do it with your might." — Ecclesiastes 9:10

"Failure is not the outcome. Failure is not trying." — Sara Blakely, interview

"She considers a field and buys it; with the fruit of her hands she plants a vineyard." — Proverbs 31:16

"Simplicity is ultimately a matter of focus." — Ann Voskamp, One Thousand Gifts

"The hand of the diligent will rule, while the slothful will be put to forced labor." — Proverbs 12:24

"The self can't be both the problem and the solution." — Alisa Childers, Live Your Truth and Other Lies

"When God says go forward, don't even think about standing still." — Attributed to Beth Moore

WORK & PURPOSE: PUTTING IT INTO PRACTICE

Write down what you think you were made to do — even if you can't fully articulate it. — One page. In pencil if you have to. Messy is fine. What matters is getting it out of your head and onto paper where you can look at it.

Identify one lie you have believed about work — and reject it this week. — "I need to hustle constantly." "My paycheck is my worth." "I can't have a family and a real career." Name it. Reject it. Replace it with the truth.

Pray over your work for thirty days. — Before the day starts. For the colleagues. For the clients. For the decisions. Just thirty days. See what shifts in you.

Have one honest conversation about money this week. — With your spouse, if you are married. With yourself, if you are not. Where is it going? Is it being stewarded? What needs to change?

Identify one skill you have been avoiding developing — and take the first step. — Negotiation. Public speaking. Finance. Technology. Whatever has been out of reach. Find one resource. Start this week.

Mentor someone younger — or ask someone older to mentor you. — If you have been in the field ten or more years, reach out to a younger woman. If you have not, reach out to an older one. Start the conversation this month.

List the ordinary work you do — and reframe one item as worship. — The laundry. The dishes. The emails. The reports. Pick one. This week, do it as unto the Lord. See what changes.

Evaluate honestly: are you in a workplace that is costing more than it is paying? — Not just financially. Relationally. Spiritually. Emotionally. If yes, begin praying about the next season. Do not panic. But begin asking.

Give something away this week that you could have kept. — Money. Time. Credit. Opportunity. Practice the generosity that keeps ambition from becoming idolatry.

Write down three things you hope your work will have built twenty years from now. — Not the title. The substance. What you want to have contributed. What you want to have left. Post it somewhere you will see it. Work toward it.

CATEGORY SEVEN

Physical Discipline

❦

List 1: Ten Truths About a Woman's Body the World Will Not Tell Her

Her body is not the enemy. — The culture has trained women to wage war against the very frame that carries them. The scale, the mirror, the dressing room — all battlefields. But the body is not an adversary to be conquered. It is a dwelling. It is the house she has been given to live in for the length of her life. The war was never the assignment. Stewardship was. The woman who stops fighting her body and starts living in it has recovered something the world tried to take.

Her body was designed for something. — Not for display. Not for decoration. Not for the consumption of strangers on a screen. Her body was designed to move, to work, to carry, to create, to rest, to endure, to last. The design is brilliant and specific and good. She does not have to apologize for any part of it. She has to learn what it was made for and honor the design.

Her body is not a before-and-after project. — The culture sells her the lie that she is perpetually unfinished — that the body she has now is merely the draft of the body she should have. Six weeks from the wedding. Three months until summer. Twelve weeks to the revenge body. She is always on her way to being someone else. She is not. She is already her. The body she has today is the body her life is being lived in — and it deserves care, not condemnation.

Her body will change — and that is not a failure. — Puberty changes it. Marriage changes it. Childbirth changes it. Motherhood changes it. Perimenopause changes it. Menopause changes it. Grief changes it. Joy changes it. Time changes it. The woman who treats every change as a crisis will spend her life in grief. The woman who accepts change as the body doing what bodies do will spend her life at peace inside her own skin.

Her beauty is not a competition. — There is no podium. There is no judge. The culture invented the comparison and then made her compete in it. She does not have to. Another woman's beauty does not diminish hers. Another woman's body does not rebuke hers. There are as many beautiful women in the world as there are women. The woman who opts out of the competition does not become less beautiful. She becomes free.

Her body is private before it is anything else. — The feed has blurred the line between what is hers and what is public, but the line was always there. Her body belongs first to her, then to her husband if she is married, then to her family in the ordinary ways bodies are known within families — and to no one else. The stranger on the internet has no claim on it. She does not owe the world access. What she does not show is not what she has been denied. It is what she has kept.

Her body does not have to be optimized to be honored. — The wellness culture has turned the body into a project with metrics — sleep scores, recovery scores, step counts, resting heart rate, ring color. Some of this is useful. Much of it is a new form of the old obsession. She can honor her body without tracking it. She can care for it without quantifying it. The data is not the discipline. The living is.

Her body carries her history. — The scar from the surgery. The stretch marks from the pregnancy. The softness where she used to be hard. The hardness where she used to be soft. The gray at her temple. The line around her eye. Every mark is a record of something she lived through. The culture sells erasure. The Lord calls it testimony. She does not have to erase her own history to be lovely.

Her body will outlast some of what she now worries about. — The thing she is anxious about today — the ten pounds, the cellulite, the wrinkle, the sag — will not matter in thirty years. What will matter is whether she still has the mobility to play with her grandchildren. Whether her back is strong enough to carry groceries. Whether she can still walk the trail she loved. She invests in the woman she will be at seventy, not the woman she wants to be on Instagram at thirty-five.

Her body belongs to the Lord. — Before it belonged to anyone else. Before the world told her what to do with it. Before the scale had a number on it. Before the mirror had a verdict. The body was made by God and given to her on loan. She is the steward. She is not the owner. And the steward's job is to care for what was given — not to hate it, not to worship it, but to tend it with the reverence due to a gift from a good Father.

List 2: Ten Lies About Her Body She Must Stop Believing

"If I were thinner, I would be happier." — The thinner woman is not happier. The thinner woman is thinner. There is a population of women who have achieved the body they wanted and discovered the misery did not leave. The misery was never about the body. The misery was the mind the body carried around. She works on the mind.

"I will start living when the body is right." — She will not. The life she is postponing is the only one she has. The beach trip she is skipping until she is a different size. The dance she is not attending until she is smaller. The photograph she is not appearing in until she is better. These are not preparations for living. These are the life itself, and she is watching it pass from the sidelines. Show up. In the body you have. Today.

"The number on the scale is a verdict on my worth." — It is not a verdict. It is a measurement. It measures gravity acting on mass. That is all. It does not measure kindness, creativity, courage, faithfulness, intelligence, humor, devotion, or love. The scale has no jurisdiction over her soul. She has given it authority it does not deserve. She can revoke that authority today.

"My body is ruined because of pregnancy." — The body that carried a child is not ruined. It is a body that performed one of the most extraordinary acts a human body can perform. The softness, the marks, the changes — these are evidence of creation, not evidence of damage. The culture has sold her the lie that the body before the baby was the real body and the body after is the compromise. That lie is backward. The body that gave life is the body that did something her pre-pregnancy body could not do.

"I am too old to get strong." — She is not. The research is clear. The body responds to strength training at every age — at fifty, at seventy, at eighty. The woman in her sixties lifting weights for the first time is building muscle, protecting bone, and extending the years she will have mobility. The age excuse is a thief. It steals the second half of her life. She refuses it.

"I have to earn food." — She does not. Food is not a transaction that requires payment in exercise. It is sustenance. The workout is not a penance. The meal is not a reward. She eats because she is a body that needs to be fed. She moves because she is a body that needs to move. The two are not in negotiation. They are both gifts.

"My body is public property because of the internet." — It is not. The feed has created the illusion of public access, but access is not a right. She does not owe the internet a photograph. She does not owe the comment section an explanation. She does not owe any stranger a justification for how she looks. What she posts is what she chose to post. Everything else is hers.

"I need to hate my body to change it." — She does not. Self-hatred is a terrible fuel. It burns short and leaves ash. The woman who cares for her body from a place of hatred will abandon the care the moment the hatred tires. The woman who cares for her body because she honors it will continue long after the motivation fades. Love builds more than hate ever did.

"Beauty is a young woman's currency." — It is not. Beauty matures. The face at sixty carries a depth the face at twenty cannot fake. The woman who has loved, labored, wept, forgiven, held, buried — her beauty is not in spite of what she has lived. It is because of it. The culture sells her the lie that her beauty expires. The Lord calls a woman of valor far more precious than rubies and does not mention an age.

"Discipline is deprivation." — It is not. Discipline is the framework that makes the good life possible. The disciplined body is not a body that has given up joy. It is a body that has traded fleeting pleasure for lasting strength. It is not less. It is more — more energy, more capacity, more years, more presence with the people she loves. Discipline is generosity. She stops confusing it with punishment.

List 3: Ten Ways to Build Strength Without Building an Idol

Start where you are. — The woman who waits to be in shape before she starts training will never start. The beginning is awkward. The beginning is humbling. The beginning is the only way to get past the beginning. She begins today, in the body she has, with whatever she can do. Tomorrow she does a little more.

Choose strength over smallness. — A generation of women was sold the pursuit of shrinking. Smaller, smaller, smaller. That pursuit has ended in fragility, in broken bones at sixty, in frailty at seventy. She chooses differently. She trains to be strong — to carry what she has to carry, to stand when she has to stand, to live the long life that is still in front of her.

Move for function, not for aesthetics. — The body she is building is the body that will still work in twenty years. The squat that keeps her getting off the floor when she is ninety. The press that lets her lift her grandchild. The deadlift that protects her back. The aesthetic will take care of itself. The function is the point.

Lift. Actually lift. — The myth that weight training will make her bulky is a myth. The woman who lifts heavy things becomes strong, lean, and capable. She does not become a bodybuilder by accident. She becomes a woman whose body does what she asks of it. Every woman should know the feeling of moving weight she did not think she could move. Every woman.

Let rest be part of the training. — The culture sells constant intensity. The body rebuilds during rest. The woman who trains without recovering is not training harder — she is training worse. She honors the rest day. She honors the sleep. She honors the deload week. The rest is not a concession to weakness. It is where the strength is built.

Train consistently — not intensely. — The woman who trains four times a week for a decade will be stronger than the woman who trains seven times a week for three months and burns out. Consistency beats intensity over a life. She chooses the pattern she can keep when she is tired, when she is busy, when she is grieving, when she is joyful. The pattern that lasts is the pattern that works.

Stop comparing your training to someone else's highlight reel. — The woman on the screen is showing her best lift of the year. You are comparing it to your Tuesday. That is not a fair comparison. Her life is not your life. Her body is not your body. Train for you, compete with yesterday-you, and close the app.

Let the training serve your life — not the other way around. — The workout that makes her a worse wife and a worse mother is not a good workout. The training that isolates her, drains her, and replaces her relationships with a gym is training that has become an idol. She keeps the body a tool for the life. She does not let the body become the life.

Pray about your training. — The body is not a secular zone. The training is not outside the Lord's concern. She can consecrate the workout the way she consecrates the meal. She can ask him for strength as she asks him for wisdom. The sweat, when offered up, is not vanity. It is stewardship.

Train so that you can serve. — The strong body is a tool of service. She can carry her children. She can carry her aging parents. She can help her neighbor move. She can go where the help is needed. The strength is not for her own reflection. It is for her household, her community, her calling. She trains so that she can give.

List 4: Ten Truths About Eating as a Steward --- Not a Prisoner

Food is a gift — receive it with thanks. — She does not owe food her guilt. She does not owe the meal her anxiety. The Lord provides food so that bodies can live. She receives it, gives thanks, and eats. The meal is not a moral event. It is a daily provision. She eats it the way she was meant to.

The body needs to be fed. — A generation of women has learned to be afraid of feeding themselves. Hunger is not a crisis to be solved with discipline. Hunger is a message to be answered with food. She does not ignore her hunger. She does not punish it. She responds to it, the way a good steward responds to any signal her body sends.

Eat foods that were food within a generation of your grandmother. — The ingredients she could name. The foods that grew, walked, swam, or came from a tree. The meals her grandmother would have recognized. This is not about purity. It is about proximity to what the body was designed to be fed.

Cook more than you purchase. — The woman who knows her way around a kitchen has a powerful form of independence. She can feed her family, her guests, herself. She controls what goes in. She tastes her own work. The woman who has abdicated cooking to convenience has given away something important. She can reclaim it.

Let the table be a sacred place. — The meal is not fuel consumed alone in front of a screen. It is a gathering. It is where the day is talked about, where the children learn to converse, where the marriage is nourished. She protects the table. She eats with her people when she can. The table is worth defending from the feed.

Stop moralizing food. — Food is not good or bad. The cake is not a sin. The salad is not a virtue. Food is food. The woman who has built an entire moral universe around what she eats has made food a theology, and food is a terrible god. She eats with pleasure, with attention, with thanks — and she lets go of the ledger.

Honor your body's signals. — When it is hungry, feed it. When it is full, stop. When it craves something specific, consider what is underneath the craving. The body speaks. The woman who has trained herself to ignore its voice has trained herself out of a conversation she needs. She listens again.

Feed yourself as well as you feed others. — The woman who will prepare a beautiful meal for her family and then eat crackers over the sink has not understood her own worth. She is worth the same care she gives the people at the table. She makes herself a plate. She sits. She eats.

Teach your children that food is joy — not fear. — The anxiety about food is transmitted at the table. The mother who polices every bite is teaching her daughter to police her own bites for forty years. She models a different relationship. Food received with thanks. Food shared with pleasure. Food that sustains and does not threaten.

Do not outsource your eating to the algorithm. — The internet has made food a content genre. The woman who takes her cues about what to eat from influencers has handed her body over to strangers with motives she cannot see. She eats what the body needs. She eats what her grandmother would have fed her. She does not need a stranger to tell her whether she is allowed to have bread.

List 5: Ten Ways to Rest Without Guilt

Understand that rest is commanded — not negotiated. — The Sabbath is not a suggestion. It was written into the foundations of creation. The woman who has never stopped has not achieved more. She has only worn herself thinner. Rest is a commandment, which means the refusal to rest is not discipline — it is disobedience dressed as devotion.

Sleep like it matters — because it does. — The body repairs itself during sleep. The mind consolidates during sleep. The hormones regulate during sleep. The woman who treats sleep as the first thing to sacrifice has sacrificed the foundation of everything she is trying to build. She protects her sleep the way she protects her time with her husband. It is not optional.

Take the day off without apology. — The Saturday she does not work. The Sunday she actually keeps. The vacation she does not check her email on. The woman who cannot take a day off without guilt has made her work an idol. She steps away from the altar. She lets the work wait. The work survived the night before her. It will survive a day.

Rest is not laziness. — The cultural confusion between the two has broken a generation of women. Laziness is the absence of effort when effort is required. Rest is the presence of stillness when stillness is required. These are opposites. She does not owe the world perpetual motion. She owes the world the person she is when she is replenished, and that woman requires rest.

Stop working at night. — The after-dinner hours were not made for checking email. They were made for the husband, the children, the book, the conversation, the sleep. The woman who cannot stop working at night is the woman whose boundary has collapsed. She builds it back. The laptop closes at a time. The phone goes in a drawer. The night belongs to her life.

Nap without shame. — The twenty-minute nap is not a failure. It is a gift the body is offering her. The woman who has learned to nap — briefly, strategically — has added years to her energy. She does not need to apologize for closing her eyes at two in the afternoon. She is human. Humans rest.

Let the house be imperfect sometimes. — The dishes can wait until morning. The laundry can sit folded. The floor does not have to be swept tonight. The woman who cannot rest until the house is perfect is the woman whose house will never be done and whose rest will never come. The house is not her god. Her family is not the housekeeping. She sits.

Rest from the feed. — The scroll is not rest. It is a different kind of work — consumption without production, which the mind experiences as exhaustion. She rests from the screen as she rests from the kitchen. She puts the phone down. She reads the book. She looks out the window. She lets the mind be quiet.

Rest in the presence of people who restore you. — Not everyone restores. Some people drain her even when they are not working her. She notices which friendships feed her and which tax her. She rests in the feeding ones. The taxing ones she manages differently. Her rest is not infinite. She spends it wisely.

Rest in the Lord before you rest in anything else. — The deepest rest is not physical. The body can sleep while the soul thrashes. The woman who has learned to cast her cares on the Lord sleeps differently than the woman who has not. She prays before bed. She reads a psalm. She surrenders the day. The soul that rests in God rests fully — and only that soul rests fully.

List 6: Ten Lies About Beauty and Aging

"Youth is the peak — everything after is decline." — This is the lie the culture sells to every woman over thirty-five. It is a lie. The woman at fifty knows things the woman at twenty-five could not know. The face at sixty has learned to laugh at more and fear less. The peak was never the smooth skin. The peak is the life lived, and she is not past it. She is in it.

"She must erase the years to be lovely." — The filler, the injection, the procedure, the filter. The woman who is erasing her face is not becoming more beautiful. She is becoming less visible. The face she was going to have at sixty — her mother's face, her grandmother's face, the face her children were going to recognize — is being traded for a face no one will remember. She can choose differently.

"Gray hair is surrender." — It is not. It is arrival. The woman who stops coloring is not giving up. She is saying something true about where she is. There is a gravity to silver hair that no dye can duplicate. She decides for herself — but she rejects the idea that going gray is a failure to maintain.

"The wrinkle is a wound." — It is not. It is a record. The line around her eye is the smile that made it. The line on her forehead is the thought that made it. The line beside her mouth is the laughter that made it. A face without wrinkles is a face without history. She has a history. Her face is supposed to show it.

"She has to compete with women half her age." — She does not. She is not in the same market. She is not even playing the same game. The forty-five-year-old who is trying to look twenty-five has chosen a losing contest. The forty-five-year-old who looks exactly like a wise, well-kept forty-five-year-old is unassailable. She is exactly what she is. She refuses to be anything else.

"Aging is a problem to be solved." — It is not a problem. It is the process of being alive. The woman who is fighting her own age is fighting the gift of years. The alternative to aging is not eternal youth. The alternative to aging is death. She chooses the aging. She chooses it gratefully.

"Her beauty is for the world — not for her husband." — The beauty that is curated for strangers on the feed and neglected for the one man who actually sees her daily has been inverted. The husband does not need her to be twenty. He needs her to be present. She cares for her appearance because she honors herself and him — not because she is auditioning for the internet.

"The skincare is the spirituality." — It is not. The culture has made wellness into a religion, and the altar is the bathroom sink. The ten-step routine will not save her soul. The retinol will not forgive her sins. She can care for her skin — she probably should — but she does not confuse the serum with the Savior.

"When she is no longer young, she is no longer seen." — The women who believe this become invisible. The women who reject it do not. The fifty-year-old who walks into the room with her head up and her voice clear is seen. Not as a twenty-year-old. As herself. And the self she has become is a presence no twenty-year-old can match.

"Her mother aged badly — so she will too." — Maybe. Maybe not. Genetics are real, but they are not fate. The habits matter. The sleep matters. The sun matters. The stress matters. The joy matters. The prayer matters. She can age well even if her mother did not. She does not inherit her mother's anxiety about the mirror.

List 7: Ten Truths About the Body After Childbirth, Illness, and Change

The body that carried life is a different body than the body before. — And that is not a tragedy. The body has been rewritten by what it has done. The core, the hips, the abdomen, the chest — all have changed. She does not expect them to go back. She does not need them to. The body she has now is the body that did something.

Recovery is not failure. — The months after birth, after surgery, after illness — these are not wasted months. They are construction months. The body is rebuilding. The mind is adjusting. The soul is catching up. She does not rush the recovery to prove something. She lets it take what it takes.

The postpartum body is not the problem the internet made it. — She is told to get her body back. The body did not go anywhere. It is here, doing an enormous job, often on no sleep, keeping a new human alive. It deserves reverence, not rebuke. The "before" body was not stolen. The body simply did something, and now it is carrying the evidence.

Scars are testimony. — The C-section line. The lumpectomy scar. The incision from the gallbladder. The mark from the accident. Each is a line of a story. She does not have to hide them. She does not have to perform acceptance of them, either. She lives inside them, and over time they become simply part of the landscape of her skin.

Chronic illness changes the math. — The body that used to run five miles now walks one. The body that used to lift heavy now moves carefully. The woman with a chronic condition is not failing at discipline. She is practicing a harder discipline — the discipline of stewarding a body with limits she did not choose. Her discipline is larger than the well woman's. It is just measured differently.

Hormones are not her imagination. — Perimenopause is real. Postpartum is real. Thyroid imbalance is real. The woman who is told to will herself through biochemistry has been failed by someone who should have helped. She does not gaslight herself. She gets the bloodwork. She finds the right doctor. She treats what is treatable.

The body does not owe her a return to a previous version. — The high school body is not coming back. The pre-baby body is not coming back. The pre-illness body may not come back. She stops waiting for it. She meets the body she has now, asks what it can do, and builds from there.

The weight that will not leave is not a moral failure. — The body holds weight for reasons — hormones, medications, stress, grief, age, genetics. She can continue to steward well without achieving a number she has been told to achieve. The scale is not her judge. Her body is not her enemy because it kept the weight. It is her body. It kept itself alive.

There is grief in a body that has changed — and the grief is allowed. — She does not have to pretend she is fine. The body that used to dance. The body that used to run. The body that used to wear the dress. It is permissible to miss the previous body. Grieve it. Name it. Then turn toward the body you have now and learn to love it too.

Every body can be honored — regardless of its current capacity. — The wheelchair does not disqualify a body from dignity. The scar does not erase it. The illness does not cancel it. Every body is a body. Every body deserves care. She extends to her own body the reverence she would extend to a body she loved.

List 8: Ten Ways to Break Up With the Scale --- and Other Measurements That Do Not Serve Her

Ask what the scale has done for your soul. — Decades of weighing in. Thousands of mornings of standing on that small square. Has she become more peaceful? More confident? More free? Or has the scale been a tyrant she has been paying rent to? She is allowed to ask. She is allowed to answer honestly.

Put the scale in the closet for a month. — Not forever. Just a month. See how her body feels. See how her mornings go. See whether the world ends. It will not. She may find the month without a daily number is a month with more actual living in it.

Measure something else. — Can she walk farther? Can she lift heavier? Does her back hurt less? Does she sleep better? Does she have more energy at three in the afternoon? These are measurements that matter to her life. The scale measures gravity. She measures flourishing.

Stop reading the tag in her clothes. — The size on the label is not a verdict. Sizing is inconsistent across brands. A ten in one store is a fourteen in another. The size has no jurisdiction over her self-worth. She buys what fits and lives in it. The tag gets cut out if it bothers her.

Stop photographing her body for evidence. — The progress photo can become a prison. Every morning she reviews herself for change. She is not a science experiment. She is a woman living a life. She can know her body without documenting it daily.

Reject the ring, the watch, the tracker — if they have become the master. — The wearable was supposed to help. For some women it does. For others it has become a source of daily anxiety. If the device is making her life worse, the device is not earning its place. She takes it off. She trusts her body to report to her without a notification.

Unfollow the accounts that make her feel worse. — The fitness influencer whose body she will not have. The wellness coach whose protocol she cannot sustain. The before-and-after account whose every post makes her compare. She unfollows. Not because they are wrong. Because their content is not serving her life.

Stop reading the comment section on your own body. — The comments on her post. The thing her aunt said at Thanksgiving. The remark from the coworker about whether she looks tired. She lets these pass through without taking up residence in her head. Their opinion of her body is not information. It is noise.

Stop confessing food to other women. — "I was so bad today." "I shouldn't have." "I only had a little." The way women talk to each other about food is a small civilization of shame. She stops participating. She does not confess her lunch. She does not ask absolution for her dessert. She eats, and she moves on.

Trust that honoring her body will produce the outcomes that matter. — The sleep. The movement. The eating. The rest. The prayer. If she does these for a decade — not perfectly, just consistently — her body will tell the truth about what it is. She does not need the metrics to prove it. She will feel it.

List 9: Ten Ways to Practice Physical Discipline Without Self-Hatred

Operate from love, not from disgust. — The training that comes from hating the body cannot last. The training that comes from loving the body can. She reframes every workout, every meal, every night of sleep as an act of care — not an act of punishment. The shift in motivation changes the shift in practice.

Talk to your body the way you would talk to your daughter's body. — She would never tell her daughter that her thighs are disgusting. She would never tell her daughter to skip dinner because of a photograph. She would never tell her daughter to hate her face. She speaks to herself the way she would speak to the girl she loves most — because she is that girl, grown up.

Celebrate small consistency — not dramatic transformation. — The week she walked every day. The month she slept well. The quarter she cooked at home more than she ate out. These are the wins. The Instagram transformation is not the goal. A life of small, consistent honoring is. Celebrate it.

Release the all-or-nothing framework. — The woman who eats one thing she considers "bad" and decides the day is ruined will eat herself into misery. The woman who eats one thing and continues her life the way it was will eat herself into health. One meal is not a failure. One meal is one meal. She continues.

Give the body credit for what it has survived. — The illnesses. The pregnancies. The accidents. The stresses. The hard years. The body has carried her through things her mind barely remembers. It deserves gratitude, not resentment. She gives it the credit. She gives it the rest.

Let the mirror be a window — not a courtroom. — The mirror shows what is there. It does not issue a verdict. She can look at herself without sentencing herself. She can notice without condemning. The mirror is a tool for checking whether her shirt is straight. It is not a judge.

Find a form of movement you actually enjoy. — The woman who forces herself into a form of exercise she hates will quit. The woman who finds something she loves will continue for decades. Walk. Swim. Lift. Dance. Ride. Whatever it is, find it. Movement she loves is movement she sustains.

Move with other women — or move alone, whichever serves you. — Some women flourish in group classes. Some women need solitude to restore. She knows herself. She does not force herself into a social fitness culture that depletes her. She does not force herself into solitary routines if community is what she needs. She moves in the way that serves her life.

Do not confuse discipline with punishment. — Discipline is steady care. Punishment is retaliation for a perceived offense. The workout is not punishment for the meal. The meal is not a reward for the workout. The practices are consistent because they serve the life — not because they balance out her guilt.

Entrust the outcome to the Lord and keep doing the work. — She will not control every outcome. Her genetics, her age, her circumstances — much of this is outside her control. What she controls is the faithfulness of her practice. She shows up, day after day, with love. The outcome belongs to God. The practice belongs to her.

List 10: Ten Things a Daughter Learns From Watching Her Mother's Relationship With Her Body

She learns whether a woman is allowed to rest. — If her mother works until she collapses, her daughter learns that women do not stop. If her mother takes the afternoon off, puts on a movie with her, and rests unapologetically, her daughter learns something different. The daughter's future pace is being set.

She learns whether food is fear or gift. — The daughter watching her mother eat is learning the relationship she will have with her own plate. If her mother eats with anxiety, with confession, with restriction, the daughter will inherit the anxiety. If her mother eats with pleasure, with thanks, with ease, the daughter will inherit that peace.

She learns whether a woman must be thin to be happy. — The daughter whose mother complains daily about her own body is learning that her body will never be good enough — because if her mother's body, which she loves, is not good enough, the daughter's will not be either. The mother's self-talk is the daughter's inner voice. Change the voice.

She learns whether her body is a subject for public comment. — The comments the mother tolerates about her own body — from the husband, from the mother-in-law, from the stranger — teach the daughter what comments she will tolerate about her own. The mother who shuts down the commentary teaches the daughter to shut it down too.

She learns whether aging is to be feared or honored. — If her mother panics at each birthday, if her mother fights every gray hair with terror, the daughter learns that her own future is a slow-motion horror. If her mother ages with acceptance and grace, the daughter learns that her own years will be an inheritance.

She learns whether her mother's attention was on the mirror or on her. — The hours spent on appearance are hours not spent on the child. The daughter knows. She knows whether she was looking at her mother's back — turned toward the reflection — or into her mother's face. She grows up and remembers which one.

She learns what a strong woman looks like. — The mother who is strong — not just aesthetically lean, but capable, muscular, confident in her own power — gives her daughter a template. The daughter grows up knowing women lift, build, endure. She does not inherit fragility as a feminine virtue.

She learns whether pregnancy ruins a body or honors it. — The mother who spent the pregnancy in grief over her changing body teaches her daughter to dread motherhood. The mother who spent the pregnancy in reverence teaches her daughter that her body is being trusted with something sacred. Prepare her to receive it as sacred.

She learns whether her body belongs to her — or to the world. — The mother who modeled modesty, privacy, and agency teaches the daughter to guard her own. The mother who performed her body online every day teaches the daughter that a woman's body is for display. Teach her agency. Teach it early.

She learns that she was loved before she was beautiful. — The daughter who has been loved for her mind, her soul, her character — not just her face — has been given an inheritance that cannot be stolen. The world will try to tell her she is only her looks. Her mother has already told her something truer. She will remember. She will draw on it for the rest of her life.

PHYSICAL DISCIPLINE: QUOTES WORTH REMEMBERING

"Do you not know that your bodies are temples of the Holy Spirit?" — 1 Corinthians 6:19

"For we are God's handiwork, created in Christ Jesus to do good works." — Ephesians 2:10

"The more intense the pain, the closer His embrace." — Joni Eareckson Tada, A Place of Healing

"I praise you because I am fearfully and wonderfully made." — Psalm 139:14

"I'm real where it counts, and that's on the inside." — Dolly Parton, interview, 1977

"Physical training is of some value, but godliness has value for all things." — Adapted from 1 Timothy 4:8

"Christianity assigns the human body much richer dignity and value." — Adapted from Nancy Pearcey, Love Thy Body

"So, whether you eat or drink, or whatever you do, do all to the glory of God." — 1 Corinthians 10:31

"God does not heal as a side gig. God is a healer." — Harris Faulkner, Faith Still Moves Mountains

PHYSICAL DISCIPLINE: PUTTING IT INTO PRACTICE

Write down what your body has carried you through. — One page. List the illnesses, the pregnancies, the stresses, the long days, the long nights, the recoveries. See the body not as an enemy but as a faithful servant. Begin there.

Put the scale in the closet for thirty days. — Not forever. Thirty days. See what happens to your mornings, your energy, your peace. Measure something else during the month — how you feel, how you sleep, how you move. See whether the number was helping you.

Start a form of strength training this week — or recommit to one. — If you have never lifted, begin with simple bodyweight movement. If you lift already, add one more session this week. Build strength you can use — for your life, your family, your longevity.

Cook one real meal for yourself this week. — Not for the family. For yourself. Set the table. Light a candle if you like. Sit down. Eat it with attention. Receive it as the gift it is.

Unfollow five accounts that make you feel worse about your body. — Today. Without an argument. Without an announcement. Just unfollow. Free your feed from the voices that are not serving you.

Stop confessing food to other women for a month. — No "I shouldn't have." No "I was so bad." No "I really only had a little." Just eat. Let food stop being a moral event. See what the silence teaches you.

Honor a full Sabbath this week. — Twenty-four hours. No work. No shopping. No striving. Worship. Eat. Nap. Read. Walk. Be present with people you love. Protect it like the gift it is.

Write a letter to your body. — Thank it. Forgive it. Make peace with it. Tell it what you will do differently. Seal it. Keep it. Read it on a day when you need to remember.

Speak about your body in front of your daughter — or a young woman you influence — the way you want her to speak about hers. — For one week, watch your words. Change what needs to change. She is listening. Give her a different inheritance.

Entrust your body to the Lord in prayer this week. — Not to be fixed. Not to be changed. Just to be received as his. Thank him for it. Offer it back to him for the work he has for it. Trust that the body he made is one he loves.

CATEGORY EIGHT

Mental & Emotional Strength

List 1: Ten Marks of a Mentally Strong Woman

She does not need every person to like her. — The mentally strong woman has made peace with the fact that she will be misunderstood by some, disliked by some, and criticized by some — and that none of this is a verdict on her worth. She does not organize her life around avoiding disapproval. She organizes her life around being the woman she was called to be. The opinion of the room does not get to overturn the opinion of her conscience.

She can sit with discomfort without fleeing it. — The mentally strong woman does not need to numb the hard feeling. She does not reach for the drink, the scroll, the snack, the shopping cart every time she is uncomfortable. She can let grief be grief, anger be anger, loneliness be loneliness. She has learned that feelings are not emergencies. They are weather. They pass.

She does not outsource her emotional regulation to her husband, her children, or her friends. — It is not her husband's job to make her happy every hour. It is not her children's job to make her feel important. It is not her friends' job to manage her moods. She manages her own inner life. The people she loves are companions in her life — not staff responsible for her well-being.

She knows the difference between a feeling and a fact. — The feeling says she is unloved. The fact is that she is loved. The feeling says she is failing. The fact is that she is doing the work. The feeling says everyone is against her. The fact is that no one is. She has learned not to confuse the two, because feelings are real but they are not always truthful.

She does not confuse processing with wallowing. — There is a time to feel a thing and a time to stop feeling it. The mentally strong woman can tell the difference. She lets the emotion do its work and then she gets up. She does not build a residence in her own pain. She honors it, and she moves through it.

She can be alone without being lonely. — Some women cannot stand their own company. They need the podcast, the show, the call, the conversation — constantly. The mentally strong woman has made peace with her own silence. She can walk alone, eat alone, drive alone, sit with her coffee alone, and not require the continuous buzz of other people to feel like herself.

She does not rehearse resentments. — She does not mentally replay the old offense. She does not keep the slight alive in her head for years. She has learned that rehearsal is rebuilding — every time she replays it, she reinforces it. She names the wrong, she grieves it, and then she stops rehearsing. Forgiveness, it turns out, is partly mental hygiene.

She can change her mind without losing her identity. — The mentally strong woman is not so fragile that a correction destroys her. She can receive a better argument, see a situation differently, realize she was wrong. Changing her mind is not weakness. It is intelligence working the way it is supposed to work. She updates her views. She does not defend them past their usefulness.

She does not perform her emotions for an audience. — The feed has turned sadness into content and grief into a caption. The mentally strong woman protects the privacy of her inner life. She may share, with her people, in her time, in her own voice. She does not broadcast her rawest moments for strangers. Her interior is not public property.

She knows when to get help. — Mental strength does not mean handling everything alone. It means being wise enough to know when the load has become too heavy for her to carry without reinforcement. The therapist. The counselor. The pastor. The doctor. The friend with the hard truth. She asks. She accepts. She recovers. The woman who is too proud to ask for help is not strong. She is stuck.

List 2: Ten Lies She Must Stop Believing at 3 a.m.

"Everyone is against me." — They are not. The catastrophizing mind of 3 a.m. builds villages of enemies out of ordinary people living ordinary lives. The coworker who did not respond to her email is not plotting her downfall. The friend who missed her text is not cutting her off. The 3 a.m. version of the world is fictional. She waits for morning.

"I am going to lose everything." — She is not. The things she has built — her family, her work, her faith, her reputation — are not about to vanish. The mind that catastrophizes at night will not catastrophize at noon. She makes no decisions at 3 a.m. She holds on and waits.

"Everyone else has it figured out — I am the only one struggling." — They do not. Every woman has a 3 a.m. At the very moment she is staring at her ceiling convinced she is the only broken one, there are ten thousand women staring at theirs convinced of the same thing. She is not uniquely broken. She is ordinarily human.

"This feeling is permanent." — It is not. Feelings are weather, not climate. The despair she feels at 3 a.m. will be diminished by 6 a.m. and tolerable by 10 a.m. She does not have to solve it tonight. She just has to get through to morning.

"I am a bad mother." — Almost certainly not. The mothers who are actually terrible do not lie awake worrying about it. The fact that she cannot sleep from the weight of caring about her children is evidence that she is not the failure the voice is accusing her of being. She reminds herself of this and closes her eyes.

"My husband does not love me." — He probably does. The man who is asleep next to her is not plotting her abandonment. He is asleep. The mind at night invents scenarios the day would never believe. She does not have the hard conversation at 3 a.m. She waits for light.

"I should have — I shouldn't have — I could have — " — The regret loop is a 3 a.m. specialty. The decisions she made years ago, replayed now under the spotlight of fatigue, look worse than they were. The past is not negotiable. The replaying is not repair. She lets it go, again, and breathes.

"God is far from me." — He is not. The feeling of his distance is not evidence of his distance. He is, at this moment, as close to her as he was in the last prayer that felt warm. He has not moved. The feeling is the fatigue talking. She whispers a psalm. She keeps breathing.

"I am behind in my life." — Behind what? Behind whom? There is no schedule. The woman who feels behind at 3 a.m. has been measuring herself against a race that does not exist. Her life is moving at the pace her life is moving. It is not a failure. It is a life.

"I cannot handle what is coming tomorrow." — She can. She has handled every day that came before. She will handle this one. Tomorrow has not arrived, and when it does, the grace will arrive with it. She does not need tomorrow's strength tonight. She needs tonight's sleep.

List 3: Ten Ways to Handle Anxiety Without Letting It Handle Her

Name the anxiety — out loud, if possible. — "I am anxious about the meeting." "I am anxious about the health thing." "I am anxious and I don't know why." The act of naming reduces the anxiety's hold. The unnamed fear is larger than the named one. She says it. She labels it. She reduces it.

Separate what is true from what is possible from what is feared. — The mind at anxious pitch collapses these categories. Something that might happen feels like something that will happen. She disentangles. She writes it down if she has to. "Here is what I know. Here is what might be. Here is what I fear." Three different columns. Three different weights.

Breathe like you mean it. — The body cannot be calm if the breath is shallow. The anxious woman has been breathing in her chest all day. She goes lower. Four seconds in, six seconds out. Again. The body reads the slower breath as safety. The system begins to settle. It is not a gimmick. It is physiology.

Get the body moving. — Anxiety sits in a still body. Walk. Stretch. Do something physical. The energy that anxiety has built has to move through. The woman who sits with anxiety in an armchair is feeding it. The woman who walks is burning it.

Cast the care on someone larger than you. — The anxious mind is a mind that has taken on responsibility that was never hers. The outcomes of the meeting, the health, the child, the marriage — none of these were hers to control alone. She gives them back. She names them and releases them. Not once. Many times. As often as they return.

Limit the intake. — The news. The feed. The doomscroll. The podcast about the end of the world. The anxious mind is not helped by more raw material. She reduces the intake. Not out of denial. Out of stewardship.

Talk to a real person — not a screen. — Text anxiety is different from phone anxiety, which is different from in-person anxiety. The in-person conversation almost always helps more. The friend. The husband. The pastor. She puts herself in the presence of another human. Something about the presence itself soothes what the screen cannot.

Move to what is true — repeatedly — even when the feeling resists. — The anxious mind invents futures that are not real. She turns to what is. The chair she is sitting in. The breath she is taking. The verse she knows. The love she has. The day she has been given. What is right now is not nothing. It is, in fact, almost everything.

Sleep, eat, hydrate, move — before you diagnose anything bigger. — Much of what feels like spiritual or emotional crisis is physical deficit. The woman who has not slept in three days is not a woman with a disorder — she is a woman who needs sleep. The woman running on coffee and stress is not broken — she is depleted. Address the basics first. Many times, the anxiety lifts.

Get professional help when it is bigger than the tools in your toolbox. — Anxiety is not a moral failure. It is not a lack of faith. It is a condition — sometimes situational, sometimes chemical, sometimes both. The therapist, the doctor, the medication — these are not the failure of faith. They are tools the Lord has provided. Use them. Do not wait until you are desperate.

List 4: Ten Ways to Feel Deeply Without Being Destroyed by the Feeling

Feeling is not weakness — it is evidence of life. — The woman who was taught to suppress her feelings to be strong was taught something untrue. Feeling is a sign that the soul is working. The mark of strength is not the absence of feeling — it is the capacity to feel without being leveled.

The feeling is visiting — it is not moving in. — Grief visits. Anger visits. Fear visits. Joy visits. They come and they go. The woman who treats each feeling as a permanent resident ends up with a very crowded house. She greets the feeling, listens to it, and lets it leave when it is ready.

Not every feeling needs to be acted on. — She can feel rage without destroying anything. She can feel fear without fleeing. She can feel despair without quitting. She can feel attraction without cheating. The feeling is information. The action is a choice. The mature woman has learned to feel fully and act wisely — two different decisions.

Let yourself cry. — There is nothing unspiritual about tears. Jesus wept. David wept. Hannah wept. The tears carry out what words cannot. The woman who has learned to cry has kept her soul from drying out. She does not apologize for them. She does not perform them. She lets them come and then she washes her face.

Write the feeling down. — The page is a safe container. What cannot be said aloud can often be written. The journal will not argue with her, will not judge her, will not correct her. It will receive her. The woman who writes out her feelings finds she has processed more than she realized.

Do not punish others for what you are feeling. — The feeling belongs to her. It is not fair to make her children pay for her anxiety, her husband pay for her grief, her coworker pay for her fear. She can feel the thing without inflicting it. This is the mark of an adult.

Do not bottle it — bottling explodes. — The woman who suppresses every feeling for the sake of seeming fine will eventually detonate. The explosion will be bigger than any honest expression would have been. She lets out small steam regularly. She does not wait until the whole system blows.

Find one person who can hold it with you. — Not everyone can. Some people panic in the face of someone else's feeling. The woman who has found one friend, one sister, one husband, one counselor who can sit with her in her hardest moment is a woman who has been given a treasure.

Do not confuse emotional intensity with spiritual depth. — The most emotional worship experience is not necessarily the most faithful. The most passionate defense of a position is not necessarily the most truthful. She has learned not to trust the feeling as her only compass. The feeling informs. The truth decides.

Bring the feeling to God — even the ugly ones. — He is not afraid of her rage. He is not offended by her grief. He is not scandalized by her fear. The Psalms are a catalog of unfiltered human feeling offered to God, and he received them. She can bring hers. She should bring hers. The feeling, offered in prayer, becomes an act of worship.

List 5: Ten Ways to Stop the Spiral Before It Starts

Recognize the early warning. — Every woman's spiral has a beginning. The thought that leads to the thought that leads to the storm. She learns her own pattern. For some, it is a text that went unanswered. For others, a weight gain of two pounds. For others, a single comparison on the feed. She catches it at the beginning.

Interrupt the pattern physically. — The spiral is a mental event, and the mind will not stop the mind. She uses the body. She stands up. She splashes cold water on her face. She walks out of the room. The physical interruption breaks the mental loop.

Put the phone down. — The phone is often the accelerant. The spiraling mind on the phone will feed itself with evidence that the world is ending. The woman who removes the phone from the spiral is a woman who has removed its best fuel.

Call someone grounded. — Not someone who will spiral with her. Someone who is steady. The friend whose voice is calm. The sister whose judgment is clear. The mother who has seen more than this. Their steadiness becomes an anchor.

Go outside. — The spiral cannot survive a walk around the block. The sky is too large for the spiral. The air is too fresh for it. The sun is too present for it. The mind that was closing in finds itself opening up. She does not underestimate how much the outside does.

Pray the specific fear out loud. — The spiral is often silent. Saying the fear out loud to God removes half its power. She does not have to pray an eloquent prayer. She can pray a sentence. "Lord, I am afraid of this." That is enough.

Refuse to engage the catastrophizing voice. — "What if — ?" "And then — " "And if that happens — " The mind will keep offering the next terrible branch. She declines to follow it. She says, out loud if necessary, "I am not going down that road." The mind will protest. It will obey.

Keep a list of evidence to the contrary. — When the spiral says she is a failure, she has a list of evidence that she is not. When the spiral says no one loves her, she has a list of evidence that they do. When the spiral says it has never been this bad, she has a list of worse times she survived. The list is not cheating. It is memory.

Eat something — sleep if you can — hydrate. — The spiral is worse when the body is depleted. Many spirals are, at their core, a blood sugar event or a sleep debt. She addresses the basics first. Often, the spiral fades.

Ask what the spiral is really about. — It is never about what it says it is about. The spiral about the email is not about the email. It is about an older fear the email triggered. She asks — gently, not aggressively — what the real issue is. When she names it, the spiral loses most of its power.

List 6: Ten Ways to Build Resilience in the Ordinary Seasons --- So It Is There in the Hard Ones

Practice faithfulness in the small things. — The resilience of a crisis is built in the small decisions of the ordinary day. The morning she got up even though she did not want to. The walk she took even though she did not feel like it. The prayer she prayed even when she did not feel heard. These are not small. These are the rehearsals.

Build habits that do not require willpower. — Willpower runs out. Systems do not. The prayer at the same time every morning. The walk at the same time every evening. The journal in the same drawer. The bible in the same place. She builds the patterns when the stakes are low so they run on their own when the stakes are high.

Know your triggers — before you are triggered. — The sound that reminds her of the trauma. The date that carries the grief. The smell that returns her to the hospital room. She knows what they are. She does not pretend they are not there. She prepares for them. She is not ambushed by them.

Have a rhythm of rest you protect fiercely. — The Sabbath. The vacation. The afternoon off. The quiet morning. The quarterly retreat. These are not luxuries. They are the practice runs for the long seasons. The woman who has learned to rest in good times has a reserve when bad times come.

Practice gratitude in the ordinary. — The woman who gives thanks for her coffee, her children, her working knees, her morning light — is a woman who is training her mind to notice good. When the storm comes, the trained mind will still notice good, even through tears. The gratitude practiced in peace becomes the gratitude that sustains in grief.

Hold onto scripture — memorize what you will need later. — The psalm you know by heart will rise in you when the wave breaks. The verse you memorized in the ordinary morning will become the verse that keeps you alive in the unbearable evening. She memorizes. She stores up the words for the day she will need them.

Build deep friendships when you do not need them — so they are there when you do. — The friendship shallow enough to need reintroduction in a crisis is not going to hold the crisis. She invests in a few deep ones over a long time. The woman who has four friends who have known her for twenty years is a wealthy woman.

Tell yourself the truth in small ways daily. — The small truth practiced daily becomes the large truth available in crisis. "I am loved." "God is with me." "This is not the end." The woman who rehearses these truths when she does not need them has them ready when she does.

Take care of the body — because the body carries the crisis. — The woman in good physical shape handles grief differently than the woman who is depleted. The sleep, the movement, the nutrition — these are not vanity. They are resilience infrastructure.

Remember how you survived the last one. — Every hard season in her past is evidence for the next one. She remembers. She recounts. She tells herself the story. "Last time, this is how I got through." The memory becomes a manual.

List 7: Ten Truths About Healing From What Was Broken

Healing is not forgetting. — She will not forget. The body remembers. The brain remembers. What was done to her is part of her history now. Healing does not erase the history. It changes her relationship to it. The woman who has healed is not a woman without a past. She is a woman at peace with a past she once thought would destroy her.

Healing is not linear. — It is not a straight line from wounded to whole. It is a spiral. She will pass through the same pain at different altitudes over the years. Each pass is different. Each pass is progress. She does not measure her healing by whether she has stopped feeling it. She measures it by how differently she meets it now.

The body keeps the score — so the body has to be part of the healing. — Trauma is physical. The cortisol, the tension, the startle response — these live in the body. Healing that is only mental is incomplete. She moves. She breathes. She rests. She does the body work alongside the soul work.

She does not have to forgive to be healed — and she does not have to be fully healed to forgive. — These are not the same process, and they do not happen on the same timeline. Forgiveness is a decision. Healing is a process. They support each other, but they are not the same. She does each at its own pace.

Some healing requires professional help. — The woman who was abused, the woman who was assaulted, the woman who was betrayed at a foundational level — she often needs more than friends and prayer. She needs a trained therapist. This is not weakness or a lack of faith. This is wisdom. The wound is too deep for self-help.

The story she tells about the wound changes as she heals. — At first, it is the whole story. Everything revolves around it. Over time, it becomes part of the story, not all of it. She becomes the woman who was wounded and healed, not just the woman who was wounded. This shift is healing in progress.

The person who hurt her does not have to participate in her healing. — He does not have to apologize. She does not need his repentance to recover. Her healing is not held hostage by his remorse. She can heal while he remains unrepentant. Her freedom does not depend on his accountability — which is good, because she may never get it.

Healed does not mean un-scarred. — The scar remains. She can press on it sometimes and feel something. This is not evidence that she is not healed. A scar is evidence of a wound that closed. The woman who has been healed is not a woman without marks. She is a woman whose marks are not bleeding anymore.

What was meant to destroy you can become what strengthens you. — Not because the pain was good. The pain was not good. But what she has done with the pain — what she has become because of it — is beyond what the pain intended. The woman on the other side of it is not less because of the wound. Often, she is more.

Jesus heals — and he heals on his timeline, not yours. — Some healings are instant. Most are not. The woman who has waited a long time for a wound to close has not been forgotten. She has been held. The long healing is not a sign of his absence. It is a sign of his patience. He is not finished with her. He will not be finished with her until he is.

List 8: Ten Truths About Depression --- And the Fight Against It

Depression is not a lack of faith. — It is a condition. It visits the faithful and the faithless. It has touched prophets and preachers, poets and pastors. The woman who is depressed is not failing spiritually. She is carrying a burden that has a name, and the name is not "unbelief."

Depression lies — and it lies with conviction. — It tells her she is a failure. It tells her she is unloved. It tells her no one would notice if she disappeared. These are lies. They are convincing, because depression is a good liar. She does not make decisions based on its claims. She waits out the lie.

The smallest acts become the heroic acts. — Getting out of bed. Brushing her teeth. Eating a meal. Showering. The depressed woman who did these today did not have a small day. She had a brave day. She records these as wins. They are wins.

Depression does not always make sense — and she does not have to explain it. — Sometimes there is a reason. Sometimes there is not. She does not owe the people around her a justification for her depression. "I am struggling" is enough. The people who love her will meet her there.

The body is part of the battle. — Sunlight. Movement. Sleep. Food. Hydration. These do not cure depression, but they support the fight. The woman in a depressive season who cannot bring herself to do the hard spiritual work can still, sometimes, take a walk. The walk is not nothing.

Medication is not weakness. — If the chemistry of her brain is producing a depression, a medication that corrects the chemistry is as appropriate as an insulin for diabetes. There is no virtue in refusing treatment. The decision is between her and her doctor — not her and the internet. She chooses wisely.

Community does not always fix it — but isolation always worsens it. — She does not expect her friends to rescue her from depression. She does expect herself to stay connected, even when depression is telling her to withdraw. The withdrawal is what depression wants. The resistance to withdrawal is what she owes herself.

God has not left her. — Even when she cannot feel him. Especially when she cannot feel him. The faithfulness of God is not measured by her emotional experience of it. He has stayed with faithful women through depression for as long as there have been faithful women. He is with her now.

This season will end. — Not on her timeline. Not as fast as she wants. But it will end. The woman who is in the middle of it feels as though it will last forever. It will not. Others have come out the other side. She will too.

Stay alive. Just stay alive. — In the worst of it, the only job is to get through to tomorrow. She does not have to solve the whole thing. She does not have to feel better. She has to stay. Tomorrow is another chance. Reach out. Tell someone. Accept help. Stay.

List 9: Ten Truths About Therapy, Medication, and Faith --- Held Together

Therapy is not confession without Jesus. — The good therapist does not replace the pastor. The good pastor does not replace the therapist. They do different work. The therapist helps her understand the mechanisms of her pain. The pastor helps her understand her place before God. The wise woman uses both.

The therapist who respects her faith is the right therapist. — Not every therapist does. The woman whose faith is central to her identity should find a practitioner who will not ask her to leave it at the door. Such therapists exist. She does not settle for less.

Medication is a tool — not a theology. — It does not mean she does not trust God. It does not mean she lacks discipline. It means she has a brain that sometimes needs help regulating chemistry. She takes it if she needs it. She titrates it with a doctor. She does not apologize for it.

Prayer is not a substitute for medical care — and medical care is not a substitute for prayer. — The woman who prays without seeing her doctor is neglecting one of God's gifts. The woman who sees her doctor without praying is neglecting the other. Both. Always both.

She does not discuss her medication with people who have not earned the conversation. — The stranger with opinions on the internet. The cousin who has a theory. The church lady who read a book. Her medication is between her, her doctor, her husband if she is married, and God. Other opinions are not owed a hearing.

Therapy is not a lifelong obligation. — It is a season. When the work is done, she can step away. She does not have to keep going out of habit. She does not have to keep going because it has become an identity. The goal of therapy is to make the therapist unnecessary. That is success.

Not every struggle is a diagnosis. — Sometimes she is sad because something sad happened. Sometimes she is anxious because something is actually worrisome. Not every painful feeling is a mental illness. The modern tendency to pathologize every emotion has its own dangers. She lets sadness be sadness sometimes.

Her family does not get a veto on her care. — The husband who is uncomfortable with therapy. The mother who thinks medication is weakness. The sister who has opinions. They do not make the medical decisions. She does, with her doctor. She loves them. But she does not let them override her care.

She can be honest with God about the struggle. — "Lord, I am depressed." "Lord, I am afraid." "Lord, I cannot feel you." This is faithful prayer. The psalmists did it. Job did it. Jesus in Gethsemane did it. Honest prayer is better than polite prayer. He is not afraid of her struggle.

She is not alone. — Not in the struggle. Not in the therapy. Not in the medication. Not in the waiting. There is a cloud of witnesses, ordinary women in every pew, who are also navigating this. She is part of a great sisterhood of the quietly struggling, and she does not have to pretend otherwise.

List 10: Ten Ways to Strengthen the Mind Daily

Read something substantial. — Not only the scroll. Not only the feed. The book. The old book, especially. The minds of the past are medicine for the mind of the present. The woman who reads substantial books is building a mind that can hold more than the moment.

Memorize something. — A psalm. A poem. A passage. The act of memorizing, in an age that has outsourced memory to the phone, is a form of mental weight training. She does it not for performance. She does it because what she carries in her head is what she has when the phone is gone.

Study something hard. — Learn the subject she has avoided. The theology, the history, the language, the skill. The brain responds to challenge. The woman who stops challenging her mind at thirty has chosen a slow mental settling. She does not choose it. She keeps learning.

Write. — The journal. The letter. The essay. The prayer. Writing forces thinking, and thinking forces clarity, and clarity is the thing the mind was built to produce. She writes regularly. Not for anyone. For herself.

Debate with yourself. — Take the position you disagree with. Argue for it fairly. See what you learn. The mind that can hold two arguments at once is a mind that has grown. The mind that can only hold its own position is a mind that is atrophying.

Get off the feed for blocks of time. — The feed is designed to fragment attention. The mind fragments along with it. The woman who reclaims hours of attention from the feed reclaims the capacity to think. She puts the phone in another room. She notices, slowly, her mind getting back its shape.

Have conversations with people who think differently than you. — Not to convince them. To understand. The woman who only talks with people who already agree with her has nothing to sharpen her mind against. She seeks out the thoughtful disagreement. She listens. She learns.

Sleep. — The mind that has not slept cannot think. Eight hours. Not a luxury. A foundation. She protects her sleep the way she protects her marriage. Her thinking depends on it.

Pray — not just for requests, but for understanding. — "Lord, give me wisdom." "Lord, help me see this clearly." "Lord, show me what I am missing." The mind opened to God is a mind with more resources than the mind closed to him. She does not approach her thinking as a secular exercise. She brings the Holy Spirit into it.

Remember that the mind is an instrument — not the self. — She is not only her thoughts. The anxious mind is not the whole of her. The doubting mind is not the whole of her. The mind is a servant. A good one, when trained. A tyrant, when untrained. She tends it. She does not worship it. She does not let it rule her.

MENTAL & EMOTIONAL STRENGTH: QUOTES WORTH REMEMBERING

"Do not be anxious about anything, but in every situation, present your requests to God." — Adapted from Philippians 4:6

"The greatest spiritual battle of our generation is being fought between our ears." — Jennie Allen, Get Out of Your Head

"Cast all your anxiety on him because he cares for you." — 1 Peter 5:7

"God is never closer than when your heart is aching." — Attributed to Joni Eareckson Tada

"Be still, and know that I am God." — Psalm 46:10

"God gives hope to all who ask Him for it. Seek Him." — Candace Cameron Bure, *Today* interview

"When I am afraid, I put my trust in you." — Psalm 56:3

"In times of pain and struggle, it's easy to question God. He is faithful." — Attributed to Shannon Bream

"The Lord is near to the brokenhearted and saves the crushed in spirit." — Psalm 34:18

"MS has the same initials as Mostly Sunny, and I take that as a sign." — Janice Dean, *Dana Perino's Book Club* interview

MENTAL & EMOTIONAL STRENGTH: PUTTING IT INTO PRACTICE

Write down three lies you hear in your own voice most often — and a true sentence to replace each. — The voice in your head is not always telling you the truth. Identify what it keeps saying. Counter it with what is actually true. Post the true sentences somewhere you will see them.

Set a 3 a.m. rule. — No hard conversations. No big decisions. No doomscrolling. When the mind spirals at that hour, reach for a psalm or a verse of scripture and wait for morning. Tell yourself tonight that you will not trust tomorrow's version of you until the sun is up.

Schedule one uninterrupted hour of real reading this week. — No phone. No screen. A substantial book. A theology. A biography. A novel. Train the attention that has been fragmented by the feed.

Memorize one passage of scripture — and start this week. — Not a verse. A passage. Psalm 23. Psalm 1. Philippians 4:4--8. Something worth having in the deep chambers of the mind. Begin on Monday. Write it on a card. Repeat it until it is yours.

Identify your early spiral warning — and commit to one interruption. — Everyone has a pattern. Yours has a beginning. When it starts, what will you do? Walk around the block. Call a specific friend. Pray a specific prayer. Decide in advance so you do not have to decide in the moment.

Talk to a professional about what you have been carrying alone. — If you have been wrestling with something for more than a season, find a qualified counselor. Just one appointment. Just to talk. Pride tells you not to go. Wisdom tells you to go anyway.

Write a letter to your younger self about what you now know is not true. — The things she feared have not happened the way she feared them. The things she thought she could not survive, she survived. The lies she believed she has outgrown. Tell her. It is also a letter to you now.

Unfollow every account that deepens your anxiety for a month. — The news that stokes panic. The influencer whose life makes yours feel small. The commentator who feeds your rage. Not forever. Just a month. See what happens to your inner life.

Build one morning habit that anchors you — and do it for forty days. — Coffee and a psalm. Ten minutes of silence. A walk before the phone. Forty days is long enough to become a pattern. Forty days is long enough to feel the difference.

Tell someone you love that you are not okay — if you are not okay. — The hardest sentence to speak is often the sentence that unlocks the most help. You do not have to explain everything. "I am struggling. I need you." That is enough to begin. Speak it to one person this week.

CATEGORY NINE

Legacy & Influence

❦

List 1: Ten Things a Woman Leaves Behind --- and What She Does Not

She does not leave behind the title. — The promotion, the rank, the corner office, the name on the door — these do not outlive her by long. Someone will take the desk. Someone will take the title. Within five years, most of the professional identity she built at such cost will have been absorbed by the next occupant. She lives for titles carefully, knowing they do not survive.

She leaves behind the people she shaped. — The daughter who learned how to love from watching her love. The coworker who kept going because of her words. The niece who figured out what kind of woman to become by watching. The neighbor whose faith was stirred by hers. These are her true inheritance — people carrying something of her forward.

She does not leave behind the things she purchased. — The house will be sold. The furniture will be divided. The wardrobe will be given away. The possessions she spent her money and attention on will scatter quickly. She does not build her life around things she will not be able to take with her and will not be able to leave in any lasting way.

She leaves behind her words. — The letters she wrote to her grandchildren. The advice she gave her daughter over the kitchen table. The prayers she whispered over her babies. The things she said that her children can still hear in her voice at forty. Words she spoke in love become a permanent recording in the hearts of the people who loved her.

She does not leave behind the injuries she inflicted if she repaired them. — The argument she lost her temper in — if she went back and apologized — does not follow her into eternity. The mistake she made — if she made it right — does not hang over her name. She is not haunted by what she was willing to repent of. Repair is the erasure she is allowed.

She leaves behind the injuries she did not repair — whether she meant to or not. — The apology never offered. The wound never acknowledged. The pattern never broken. These remain. The children who never heard her say she was sorry for the thing that marked them will carry it. She repairs what she can repair. She does not wait until she is dying to say the things that should have been said twenty years ago.

She does not leave behind the image she curated on the feed. — The archives of her social media will be forgotten within a generation — often within a decade. The performance she exhausted herself building will not be remembered. Her actual life, the one she was sometimes neglecting for the feed, is the one that will be remembered. She chooses accordingly.

She leaves behind the way she handled the hard years. — The illness. The loss. The betrayal. The collapse. The long grief. Her children will remember not the crisis itself but the way she walked through it. Her grace under fire. Her faith in the dark. The way she did not become bitter. Her response to her hardest years is the most-watched lesson of her life.

She does not leave behind the approval she chased. — The boss whose favor she lived for. The in-laws whose respect she tried to earn. The friend whose good opinion she was always working for. None of this survives. The approval was never the treasure she thought it was. She stops collecting it.

She leaves behind her faith — if she actually lived it. — The prayers her children saw her pray. The Bible she wore out. The Sunday mornings she showed up even when she was tired. The way Jesus was real to her in her ordinary days. This is the inheritance that matters most. It is also the hardest to fake, because the children who grew up with her can tell the difference.

List 2: Ten Ways to Influence Without a Platform

Be the woman they remember from Thanksgiving. — You do not need a podcast to shape a generation. You need presence at the table. The conversations around holiday meals, the laughter, the question you asked the twelve-year-old who was being ignored, the moment you listened to the uncle no one was listening to — these are influence. These are discipleship in ordinary clothes.

Write letters. — Handwritten, mailed, opened on a Tuesday when they were not expecting it. A letter from a woman to her niece, her goddaughter, her son in his first semester away from home — this is a form of influence the internet cannot match. The letter survives. The letter is reread. The letter becomes part of the recipient's story.

Show up when it is hard. — Not just the wedding. The funeral. Not just the baby shower. The hospital room. Not just the promotion. The layoff. The woman who shows up in the ugly moments becomes the woman whose influence outlives everything else. She was there. They remember. That is what matters.

Pray for people by name — consistently, over years. — The woman who prays specifically for the ten people in her world, by name, for a decade — is a woman whose influence is written in heaven whether or not anyone sees it on earth. Many of the answers she sees are answers to prayers she quietly prayed in rooms no one noticed.

Cook for someone who needs it. — A meal, brought to a door, at a hard moment — a new baby, a new grief, a new diagnosis — is a form of influence that no post can equal. The woman who feeds people when they cannot feed themselves is practicing a ministry older than the church and more lasting than most sermons.

Disciple the young women around you — informally. — You do not need a curriculum. Invite her for coffee. Ask her what she is carrying. Share what you have learned. The younger woman who has an older woman willing to pour into her is a woman with an advantage she did not earn. Be that advantage for someone.

Speak honestly in the rooms you are in. — The book club. The committee. The staff meeting. The school drop-off. You do not need a microphone. You need the courage to tell the truth in the small spaces where you are already present. Truth told in ordinary rooms has an echo the big rooms do not.

Keep your word — over years. — Do what you said you would do. Every time. The woman who keeps her promises for decades builds a kind of reputation that no marketing can match. People trust her. People bring her the important things. Her influence grows without her chasing it.

Forgive openly — and teach others how. — The woman who forgives visibly, who lets her children see her extend grace, who models it in front of her friends, is teaching something the world cannot teach. She does not perform the forgiveness. She just lives it out where people can see.

Let the Lord be obviously at the center of your life. — Not because you announce it. Because it cannot be hidden. The woman for whom Jesus is unmistakably real, in the way she talks about her life, the way she makes decisions, the way she handles fear, the way she celebrates — teaches the gospel without ever giving a lecture. Her influence is the Holy Spirit at work in her life.

List 3: Ten Ways to Make the Room Better for the Women Who Come After You

Promote them — when you have the power to do so. — The woman who makes it into the position of hiring authority and then does not use it to open doors for other women has forgotten what her own climb cost her. When you have the power, use it. Not to promote incompetent women — to promote qualified women who would not have been considered without you.

Tell the truth about what it was like. — The lies, the obstacles, the double standards, the ways you almost quit, the costs no one warned you about. The woman coming up behind you deserves the real story. Not to scare her — to prepare her. The myth of the seamless rise has to die. The honest account keeps her from thinking she is uniquely broken.

Advocate for her out loud. — In the meeting she is not in. At the table where her name comes up. In the email thread that will determine her next assignment. The woman who quietly advocates for other women when they are not in the room is doing the essential, invisible work of sisterhood. Do it.

Introduce her to people who can help her. — Your network is not a possession. It is a responsibility. The woman who has built relationships with the right people has an obligation to put those relationships into the hands of the woman who needs them. Make the introduction. Send the email. Make the call.

Write a recommendation even when you are busy. — The letter of recommendation she needs for the fellowship, the grant, the job, the program — write it, and write it well. The woman who has asked you has been working up the courage to ask. Your five pages can change her trajectory. Take the time.

Share the playbook. — The contract language you wish you had known. The salary negotiation language you use now. The way you handle the difficult meeting. The way you respond to the kind of email that used to ruin your week. Hand it to her. Do not make her reinvent what you have already figured out.

Challenge her — kindly — when she is playing small. — She is underselling herself in the interview. She is not applying for the job she is qualified for. She is letting a man take credit for her idea. You see it. Name it. Do not let her stay in a pattern that is costing her. The good mentor tells the truth.

Protect her when you can. — From the boss who is about to sabotage her. From the client who is going to burn her. From the project that is going to consume her without reward. You cannot protect her from everything. But when you see the grenade rolling toward her and you have the warning, you give her the warning.

Celebrate her publicly. — Her win. Her promotion. Her book. Her milestone. Post about it. Share it. Make sure your network knows. Many women are uncomfortable promoting themselves. You are not. You do it for her. This costs you nothing and multiplies her.

Do not compete with her — sisterhood was never a zero-sum game. — Her success is not your loss. Her rise is not your ceiling. There is room for both of you. The woman who believes scarcity has already lost. The woman who believes abundance keeps winning, and so do the women around her.

List 4: Ten Ways to Mentor Without an Agenda

Listen first. Advise second. — The younger woman who comes to you does not need you to start with solutions. She needs you to start with attention. Listen to her whole situation. Ask a question. Listen more. When you do speak, you will be speaking into a real picture, not a sketch.

Believe her when she describes what she is up against. — Do not minimize what she is facing because it was worse in your day. Her obstacles are her obstacles. She is navigating a world you did not navigate, with tools you did not have, in a market you do not fully know. Believe her description. Then help her from there.

Do not require her to become a younger version of you. — Your path is not her path. Your choices are not her choices. The woman you are mentoring is her own woman. Your job is to help her become more fully herself — not to produce a smaller copy of yourself. She will make decisions you would not make. That is not failure. That is her.

Give her the blunt truth — kindly. — The flaw she cannot see. The pattern that is costing her. The habit that will undermine her. She needs this from someone who actually loves her. Deliver it with care. But deliver it. She did not come to you for comfortable praise. She came to you for real counsel.

Share your failures — not just your wins. — The younger woman has already seen your highlight reel. She needs your bloopers. The mistakes you made. The seasons that humbled you. The decisions you regret. The woman who has been mentored by your failures is better prepared for her own than the woman who was only dazzled by your successes.

Invest before you expect. — The relationship has to be yours to give before it is hers to take from. Invest in her without expectation. Over time, the investment grows into a relationship of depth. Mentors who expect immediate returns have not understood the nature of the work.

Do not make her your project. — She is not your experiment. She is a full person with her own agency, her own God-given path, her own discernment. You are a companion, not a designer. The woman who turns her mentee into a project has crossed a line. Stay in your lane.

Release her when it is time. — At some point, she will no longer need you the way she once did. That is the goal. Do not hold her too tightly. Do not require her to keep coming back out of obligation. Let her fly. Be available. But do not be possessive.

Let her mentor you in return. — The younger woman has things to teach you. About the world you did not grow up in. About the technology you are behind on. About the cultural shifts you do not see. A wise mentor knows the relationship is not one-directional. Receive what she is giving you.

Pray for her. — Regularly. By name. For the specific things she is facing. Much of what a mentor contributes happens in the silent corners where God is being asked to do what the mentor cannot do. Do not underestimate what prayer, quietly offered for her, accomplishes.

List 5: Ten Ways to Speak Life Into the People Around You

Say the thing you are thinking about them — out loud. — The woman you admire. The friend who is doing something brave. The daughter whose character you have noticed. The coworker whose integrity you have watched. Tell them. Most of the kindest thoughts one human has about another are never spoken. Speak yours.

Write down the specific thing — not just the general compliment. — "You are a great mom" is nice. "The way you handled the conversation with your son last week — the patience, the firmness, the love — I have been thinking about it all week" is life. Specificity is what moves compliments from polite to powerful.

Tell people what you see in their children. — The things she, as their mother, may be too close to notice. "Your son is unusually kind." "Your daughter has a remarkable gift for listening." These are gifts you give the mother and the child both. Give them.

Speak well of people when they are not in the room. — The measure of a woman's integrity is not what she says to someone's face. It is what she says about them when they cannot hear. The woman who speaks well of others in their absence is the woman whose face-to-face compliments are trustworthy.

Thank people for specific things — in writing. — Not "thanks for everything." "Thank you for the way you handled Sarah's question in the meeting yesterday. You saw what I missed." The specific thank-you lands. It is remembered. It often becomes the single moment the recipient remembers from the whole year.

Tell your children, out loud and often, what you love about who they are — not just what they do. — They need to hear the being-praised, not just the doing-praised. "I love how thoughtful you are." "I love the way you notice people." Not because they are getting straight A's or winning games. Because they are becoming. Name it. They will carry it.

Praise effort as much as outcome. — The child who tried hard and lost. The friend who went for it and did not land it. The coworker who led bravely and the project failed anyway. The effort is real. Honor it. The woman who only praises winners teaches the people around her not to take risks.

Bless people at milestones. — Graduations. Weddings. Birthdays. New jobs. New houses. Do not let the milestone pass without a real word from you. Write the card. Make the toast. Send the note. The word you speak at a milestone becomes part of the person's memory of that milestone.

Tell the truth about what someone meant to you — while they can still hear it. — The mother. The father. The aunt. The mentor. The teacher. Do not wait for the eulogy. Write the letter now. Call the phone number now. Tell them what they gave you, now, while it can still land in their own life. Funerals are full of words the living could have heard.

Let your words be few — but weighted. — The woman who speaks constantly dilutes her own speech. The woman who speaks sparingly gives her words gravity. When she speaks a blessing, it lands, because it was not one of a thousand words that day. It was one of a few. Make your words rare enough to matter.

List 6: Ten Things to Pass Down on Purpose

Pass down the stories. — The story of your grandmother. The story of your mother. The story of how you met your husband. The story of the hardest year you survived. The story of how God provided. The children who grow up hearing the stories grow up in a larger house than the children who do not. Tell them often.

Pass down the recipes. — Not the ones from the magazine. The ones from your grandmother's kitchen. The ones that have been in your family for four generations. Write them down. Cook them with your daughter. Teach her not just the ingredients but the hand-feel of the dough, the smell of the moment when it is done. Recipes are a kind of inheritance.

Pass down the photographs — with names on the back. — The photos are useless if no one knows who is in them. The woman who sits with her aging mother and writes names on the back of old photographs is doing archaeology for her own children. Do it while there is still someone alive who knows.

Pass down the language — if you have one. — The Spanish. The Polish. The Korean. The German. The language that was spoken in your grandmother's kitchen. The children who inherit a heritage language inherit a door to their ancestors. Teach what you can. Sing the songs. Keep the cadence alive.

Pass down the faith — deliberately. — The Bible with your notes in the margins. The prayer you always prayed at bedtime. The verse you hung on the kitchen wall. The song you sang on hard nights. Faith is caught, not just taught, but it has to be accessible. Leave the accessible pieces.

Pass down the values — not just in lectures, in practices. — The family habit of giving to those in need. The tradition of pausing to pray together.

The way you always honor the elderly. Values that are lived are values that are inherited. Values that are only spoken about are often lost.

Pass down the books. — The ones that shaped you. Annotated. With your notes in the margins. The children who someday open your library find not just the words of the authors but the record of your engagement with them. The library you leave is a map of how you thought.

Pass down the financial wisdom. — How to save. How to budget. How to invest. How to say no to the salesman. How to live within your means. How to give generously. Many families do not talk about money. They should. The woman who teaches her daughters and sons financial wisdom has given them a form of freedom.

Pass down the family records. — The birth certificates. The marriage licenses. The military documents. The naturalization papers. The letters from the war. The deed to the farm that was sold in 1952. Put them in one place. Label them. Your children will want to know.

Pass down the names. — The names of ancestors. The middle names given in honor of someone specific. The reasons your children have the names they have. The children who know why they are named what they are named feel the weight of belonging to something older than themselves. Tell them.

List 7: Ten Ways to Let Your Children Watch You Live --- and Benefit From the Watching

Let them see you pray — not just in church. — In the car before the long drive. In the kitchen before the important conversation. Over the meal in a restaurant. Before bed on a night that was hard. The child who grows up watching her mother pray in private has absorbed that God is real in a way no Sunday school can match.

Let them see you open the Bible — on a Tuesday. — Not as a performance. Just as what you do. The Bible on the counter. The notes in the margins.

The highlighted passages. The child who sees the book being read is a child who understands the book is not ornamental. It is food.

Let them see you apologize — to your husband, to a friend, to them. — The apology modeled is the apology inherited. The child who watches her mother say, "I was wrong. I am sorry. Will you forgive me?" learns how to do it herself. The child who never sees it learns that adults do not apologize. Either lesson is permanent.

Let them see you handle disappointment. — The promotion that did not come. The friendship that ended. The hope that did not materialize. The child who watches her mother grieve honestly and recover gracefully learns something no lecture could teach. Most of life is disappointment navigated well. Model the navigation.

Let them see you forgive — even when it is hard. — The relative who hurt you. The friend who betrayed you. The person who embarrassed you in public. The child who watches her mother extend forgiveness — slowly, deliberately, truthfully — learns that resentment is not the only option. She has a model for her own life.

Let them see you work hard — and also rest. — Both. Not just one. The child who watches her mother work and never rest learns that she must never rest. The child who watches her mother rest and never work learns that work is optional. She needs both models. Give her both.

Let them see you enjoy your husband. — The laughter at the dinner table. The dance in the kitchen. The hand he puts on your back when you pass him. The inside jokes. The daughter who sees her parents' marriage modeled with joy has an image of marriage that most of her generation will not have. Gift her this image.

Let them see you weep. — When someone dies. When something hurts. When the world breaks. Do not always pretend to be okay for them. The child who has seen her mother weep and also seen her mother continue has learned that sorrow is survivable. This is one of the most important lessons childhood can offer.

Let them see you handle money. — At the store. At the checkout. At the bill-paying moment at the table. Talk through it out loud. "We don't buy this because we are saving for this." "We are giving this away because this family needs it." The child who watches money being handled thoughtfully learns a theology of stewardship.

Let them see you fail — and not give up. — The project that did not work. The business that failed. The plan that fell apart. The woman who rises back up in front of her children is a woman who has handed them the most valuable gift: an image of failure as not-final. Their own failures will not wreck them, because they saw yours not wreck you.

List 8: Ten Marks of a Woman Who Will Be Remembered Well

She was present. — Not distracted. Not always on her phone. Not perpetually somewhere else. When she was with you, she was with you. The conversation had her. The child had her. The meal had her. Her presence was a gift, and it is the single thing most often named at her funeral.

She was honest. — You could not get her to say something she did not believe. She would not flatter you. She would not perform affection she did not feel. When she told you you were doing well, she meant it. When she told you you were not, she also meant it. The honesty became a treasure because it was trustworthy.

She laughed easily. — She did not take herself too seriously. She found the absurd in her own life before anyone else did. Her laugh was memorable — a specific sound that returned to her children years after she was gone. The sound of her laugh is what they most miss.

She forgave — visibly. — She did not hold grudges. She did not accumulate wrongs. She let go of things that other women carry for decades. The release showed on her face. The children who watched her forgive learned something about freedom.

She showed up — in the ordinary and the extraordinary. — She was at the recital and she was at the hospital room. She was at the wedding and she was at the funeral. Her presence was a steady thing you could count on. You did not wonder if she would come. You only wondered what time.

She worked hard — and did not brag about it. — Her work was evident. The house, the business, the raising of the children, the care of her parents. She carried enormous loads without a performance of carrying them. The people who benefited from her work often did not know how much it cost her.

She kept her promises — over decades. — The commitment she made at twenty-five she was still keeping at seventy-five. The vow, the obligation, the word given. She did not break promises when it became inconvenient. Her word was her life, and her life demonstrated her word.

She made people feel known. — When she asked how you were, she actually wanted to know. When she remembered the thing you told her last time, she surprised you. The woman who makes people feel known is a woman whose name is spoken warmly, long after she is gone.

She loved her husband well — and stayed. — Through the hard seasons. Through the boring seasons. Through the almost-quitting seasons. She stayed and kept loving and kept building. Her marriage was not a performance. It was a partnership that held weight. Her children inherited an image of a marriage worth having.

She kept the Lord at the center — even when nothing was easy. — This is what made her, finally, what she was. Not her talent. Not her looks. Not her personality. The Lord was the reason she was kind, the reason she forgave, the reason she endured, the reason she laughed. When her children spoke of her, they spoke of the Lord. Not because she was always speaking of him. Because she was always living him.

List 9: Ten Things to Build That Will Outlive You

Build a marriage that lasts. — One marriage, well-kept, for fifty years, becomes a monument. It teaches every child who watches it. It becomes a possibility for every young woman who knew the couple. It is not a small thing. It is perhaps the greatest public service most women will render. Build it.

Build children who can love and be loved. — Not successful children by the world's metrics. Whole children. Children who can be kind, who can be honest, who can forgive, who can stay, who can show up. These children become the adults who raise grandchildren. The line of influence extends beyond what you will live to see.

Build a faith community — if you are part of one, invest in it. — A church is not a consumer product. It is a body you belong to and build together. The women who invested in their local church for forty years left behind a community. Their names are on classroom walls and in the memories of three pastors. They built something that outlived them.

Build friendships that last decades. — The friend from college. The friend from the early years of motherhood. The friend from the hard season. Invest in a few deeply. Forty years later, you will have a small council of women whose lives have grown together. This is something money cannot buy and the internet cannot duplicate.

Build a practice of generosity. — Give, consistently, for a lifetime. To your church. To the causes that matter. To the people in need in your path. The woman who has been generous for forty years has set in motion effects she will never see. Some of the children who were fed because of her giving will themselves feed others.

Build a body of work — whatever your craft is. — The book. The business. The classroom of students. The garden. The nonprofit. The home you made beautiful. The meal you cooked for twenty years. Something made, something tended, something that continues. She leaves it — and it continues without her.

Build a home that is a place of refuge. — For your family. For your friends. For the stranger. The home that is a refuge becomes the home that is remembered. Years after the children have moved out, they will come back, and bring their own children, and want their own children to know what that home feels like.

Build a prayer habit that has a history. — Years of intercession for the people in your life. A list that has been prayed over for decades. Names of the children, the grandchildren, the ones who have wandered. The woman who has prayed the same list for forty years has built something in the unseen realm whose full effect will only be known in eternity.

Build a relationship with scripture that matters. — Not a casual acquaintance. A long marriage. Year after year in the same book. Reading it, rereading it, letting it read you. The woman who has built this kind of relationship with the Bible has built a treasure that funds the rest of her life.

Build a soul that can meet God without flinching. — Everything else is subsidiary. The soul prepared for eternity is the one thing you will, in fact, take with you. She tends it. She lets the Lord tend it. She arrives at the end of her life with a soul that is ready for the real beginning.

List 10: Ten Ways to Finish Your Life With More Than You Started With

Own more peace. — Not peace as the absence of trouble. Peace as the settled confidence of a soul that knows whom it belongs to. The woman who finishes her life with more peace than she started with has made progress the world cannot measure.

Own more wisdom. — The decades are supposed to teach her something. She is supposed to know more at seventy than she did at twenty-five — not just more facts, but more of what to do with them. The wise old woman is not a character from a fairy tale. She is a role available to every woman who keeps paying attention.

Own more kindness. — The younger woman can afford to be impatient. The older woman should have worn away her rough edges. She is supposed to have become more gentle. If she has become harder over the years, she has misunderstood aging. The right direction is toward softness. Toward mercy. Toward gentleness.

Own more gratitude. — The grateful old woman is a marvel. The ungrateful old woman is a tragedy. The difference between them is not their circumstances. The difference is a daily practice pursued for forty years. She chooses. She chooses, and chooses again.

Own fewer grudges. — The woman with a list of people she still has not forgiven, at seventy, is not a strong woman. She is a burdened one. She sets them down. One by one. She finishes her life with a shorter list than she had at fifty.

Own more joy. — Joy not dependent on outcomes. Joy not tied to what is happening in the house or the country or the world. Joy that comes from the bedrock, and so is available whether the day is good or bad. The old woman's joy is a specific thing. It is witnessed. It is inherited.

Own more love. — More love for her husband than she had on her wedding day. More love for her children than she had when they were small. More love for her friends than she had when the friendship started. More love for the Lord than she had when she first knew him. Love that is deeper for having weathered.

Own more faith. — She has seen God do what he said he would do. Enough times. She has walked through enough valleys to know he has not left her. Her faith at the end should not be smaller than her faith at the beginning. It should be battle-tested and bigger.

Own fewer possessions. — By design. She has been simplifying. She has been giving away. She has been unburdening. The old woman heaped up with stuff has spent the decades wrongly. The old woman with less — because she has been handing things off — is freer.

Own the confidence that she has done what she was called to do. — Not perfectly. No one does it perfectly. But faithfully. She ran the race. She kept the faith. She poured out what she was given. She can look at her life and not flinch. That is what finishing well looks like. That is what she is building toward.

LEGACY & INFLUENCE: QUOTES WORTH REMEMBERING

"One generation shall commend your works to another, and shall declare your mighty acts." — Psalm 145:4

"A good name is to be chosen rather than great riches." — Proverbs 22:1

"I grew up believing that through God all things are possible." — Dolly Parton, multiple interviews

"The memory of the righteous is a blessing." — Proverbs 10:7

"Comparison robs us of the joy of obedience." — Jennie Allen, Restless

"A good person leaves an inheritance for their children's children." — Proverbs 13:22

"The soil from which all sin grows is unbelief." — Jackie Hill Perry, Holier Than Thou

"She opens her mouth with wisdom, and the teaching of kindness is on her tongue." — Proverbs 31:26

"I'm called to be a witness." — Harris Faulkner, Beliefnet interview

"Women of the Bible were central figures in God's story." — Adapted from Shannon Bream, The Women of the Bible Speak

LEGACY & INFLUENCE: PUTTING IT INTO PRACTICE

Write a letter to each of your children — to be opened on a specific date. — Their eighteenth birthday. Their wedding day. The day you are no longer here. Tell them what you have most wanted them to know. Do it this year. Do not put it off.

Call the older woman whose influence shaped you — and tell her so. — Before she is gone. Before you wish you had. The grandmother, the teacher, the aunt, the mentor. Make the call this week. Say what you have been meaning to say.

Identify one younger woman to pour into — and reach out this month. — Someone in your church. Someone at your work. Someone in your family. Not a program. A person. Invite her for coffee. Begin the conversation.

Write down ten stories from your life — before they are lost. — Your own childhood. Your parents' stories. Your grandparents' stories. The hard years. The surprises. The way God moved. Write them in your own voice. Give them to your children.

Organize the family photos — with names and dates. — Spend one Saturday. Label what you can. Ask your mother to help while she still can. The photo archive without names is a half-lost inheritance.

Make a list of five people you want to bless with a specific word — and do it this month. — Tell them what they have meant to you. In writing or in person. Be specific. Do not assume they know.

Identify one thing you want to build that will outlive you — and take the next step. — The book. The business. The ministry. The habit of giving. Decide what you are building. Take one step toward it this week.

Give something significant away — while you are alive to see it received. — Money. A possession. A piece of wisdom. Do not save all your generosity for your will. Hand some of it over now. The joy of giving is a joy you should experience yourself.

Sit down with an older woman in your family — and ask her to tell you the family stories. — Record it if she lets you. The moment will not come again. Do it while the storyteller is still alive.

Write your own legacy statement — what you hope will be said at your funeral. — Not vanity. Clarity. Write the eulogy you want to have earned. Then begin living the life that would make it true.

CATEGORY TEN

Faith & Spiritual Warfare

List 1: Ten Marks of a Woman Whose Faith Is Real

Her faith has been through something. — The faith of a woman who has never suffered is not yet faith in the deepest sense. It is belief. It is assent. Real faith is what she has after the betrayal, the diagnosis, the loss, the long silence. The woman whose faith is real has been in the dark and has kept walking. Her faith has the weight of a thing that has been tested.

She does not require God to make sense to her before she trusts him. — She has learned that her understanding is a small instrument and his purposes are not bound by it. She trusts him even when she does not follow the reasoning. This is not blind faith. It is faith that has looked at God's track record and decided he has earned the benefit of the doubt.

She prays like God is actually listening — because she actually believes he is. — Her prayer life is not performance. It is not a rehearsed script. She talks to him the way a daughter talks to a father who loves her. With honesty. With interruption. With the ordinary language of an ordinary day. She does not need eloquence. She needs contact.

She opens her Bible because she hungers — not because she has to. — The scripture is not a duty for her. It is a meal. She has learned that hours of feed-scrolling do not feed her soul, and ten minutes in the Psalms does. She opens the book without being forced. She returns to it because the alternative has proven insufficient.

She obeys — even when obedience is expensive. — The forgiveness she owed and finally extended. The conversation she avoided and finally had. The giving she could not afford and did anyway. The sin she walked away from at a cost. Her obedience is not theoretical. It has cost her something. It always does.

She can tell the difference between her own voice and his. — Her own voice is loud, anxious, self-protective. His voice is often quieter, steadier, more generous, more truthful. She has listened enough to know the difference. The woman who cannot tell the difference between the two has not spent enough time in the listening.

She walks with other believers — she is not a solo Christian. — She knows the pattern. Solo Christians drift. The woman whose faith is real is in a community that knows her, that challenges her, that prays for her, that notices when she is off. She does not privatize her walk with God. She knows herself too well.

She has been humbled — and remains humble. — She is not surprised by her own capacity for sin. She has seen her own heart. She is not shocked when she falls; she is grieved, and she repents, and she returns. The woman whose faith is real does not think too highly of herself. She thinks rightly of herself — which is humbly.

She extends to others the grace she has received. — The woman who has tasted real forgiveness forgives more easily. The woman who has been accepted as she is accepts others as they are. Grace is downstream water. If it is not flowing out of her, it is not flowing into her. She is a channel, not a cistern.

She hopes — even against the evidence. — The hope that the prodigal child will come home. The hope that the marriage can be restored. The hope that the calling will be fulfilled. The hope that the Lord will have the last word. The woman whose faith is real hopes when the evidence of earth says otherwise — because her hope is not grounded in earth.

List 2: Ten Lies the Enemy Whispers Specifically to Women

"You are too much." — Too loud. Too emotional. Too opinionated. Too ambitious. Too needy. Too sensitive. The enemy tells her to shrink, because he knows a shrinking woman cannot do what God made her to do. She rejects the lie. She was not made to be less. She was made to be her.

"You are not enough." — Not thin enough. Not pretty enough. Not young enough. Not smart enough. Not holy enough. Not loved enough. This lie is the twin of the last — and the enemy plays them both, depending on which will make her smaller today. She rejects this one too. Her sufficiency is not in herself. Her sufficiency is in Christ.

"Your past disqualifies you." — The thing she did at nineteen. The thing that was done to her at twelve. The years she walked away. The mistakes she cannot erase. The enemy replays her worst tape and tells her God will never use her. He is lying. The Lord uses disqualified women. The Bible is full of them.

"You are a bad mother." — The lie rises at 2 a.m. and again at 4 p.m. The critical voice that measures her against the impossible woman on the feed. The voice that tells her she is scarring her children. It lies. She is a real mother doing a real job. She is not ruining them. She is raising them.

"You will not be loved if they really know you." — So she hides. She performs. She keeps people at arm's length. The enemy's lie keeps her lonely in a room full of friends. She defies the lie. She lets one person know her. Then another. The belonging comes only when the hiding stops.

"Your life is wasted." — The way it is going. The thing you thought you would be by now. The contribution you thought you would have made. The enemy tells her the life she is in is small, dull, and beneath her. He lies. The ordinary life faithfully lived is not wasted. It is extraordinary, in the only way that will matter at the end.

"God is disappointed in you." — For the slip. For the anger. For the doubt. For the laziness. The enemy paints God as a perpetually frustrated father. The Lord paints himself as a father running down the road to meet the returning child. She takes God's self-description over the enemy's portrait.

"You are alone." — The enemy whispers this especially in the dark. Her friends have abandoned her. God has forgotten her. Her husband does not understand her. Her children do not see her. Lies, all of them. She is surrounded by a great cloud of witnesses, dwelled in by the Holy Spirit, held by a God who has sworn never to leave her.

"Your prayers are not doing anything." — The enemy wants her to stop praying. So he tells her it is useless. The marriage is not getting better. The child is not coming home. The job is not improving. She ignores the assessment. She keeps praying. Much of the real work is invisible, and the enemy knows this. Her persistence in prayer is a weapon he cannot counter.

"You can compromise on this one small thing." — The little integrity breach. The quiet participation in the gossip. The viewing of the thing you should not view. The small lie. The enemy specializes in the small compromise, because small compromises accumulate into large captures. She refuses the small compromise. The refusal protects what the enemy is really after.

List 3: Ten Ways to Fight for Your Faith When You Are Weary

Show up anyway. — To church. To prayer. To the scripture. To the community. Not because you feel like it. Not because it is working. Because faith is a long obedience, and the showing up is, in large part, the faith. Feelings return. Practice precedes them. She shows up.

Read the Psalms when the rest of the Bible feels too demanding. — The psalmist has been where she is. Worn out. Betrayed. Confused. Afraid. Angry at God. His words become her words. She does not have to generate her own prayer. She borrows his. This is what the Psalms are for. Use them.

Reach for the shortest prayer you can muster. — "Help." "Jesus." "Please." "I am here." The long, beautiful prayer can wait for another season. The weary season only requires the shortest words. He hears them. He is not offended by them. They are enough.

Let others pray for you when you cannot. — Tell a friend. Tell your pastor. Tell your small group. "I am struggling. Please pray." Do not hide it. The body of Christ was designed for exactly this moment. Your burden can be carried by others until you can carry it again yourself.

Return to the moment of your first faith. — The verse that first landed. The song that first opened you. The place where you first met the Lord. Sometimes the way forward is a revisiting. The fire that was once kindled does not die easily. She stokes it again.

Remove the distractions that are eroding you. — The feeds. The shows. The voices. The habits. Whatever is making you weary, remove what you can remove. The weary soul needs cleaner inputs. She does not have the strength, right now, for what she can tolerate in stronger seasons.

Sleep. Eat. Hydrate. Walk. — Much of what feels like spiritual collapse is physical depletion. The weary woman who has slept four hours and eaten poorly is not in a spiritual crisis. She is in a biological one. She addresses the basics first. The faith often returns when the body does.

Hold on to what you know — when you cannot feel anything. — The feelings have left. The zeal has gone. She is running on memory alone. This is fine. The feelings will return. The memory is enough for now. "I know whom I have believed." She anchors there.

Do not make major decisions in a weary season. — Do not quit the church. Do not quit the marriage. Do not quit the calling. The weary self is not your best self. She waits for stronger ground. Big decisions are for rested minds and replenished souls.

Trust that this, too, is part of the story. — The weary season is not a detour from your faith. It is part of it. Most mature believers have been through such seasons. They emerged with a deeper faith, not a lesser one. This is not the end. This is forming you into someone stronger.

List 4: Ten Habits of a Praying Woman

She prays at fixed times. — Morning, before the phone. A moment at noon. A moment at night. Fixed times remove the decision. The woman who waits to feel like praying mostly does not pray. The woman who prays because it is 6:30 a.m. — prays.

She keeps a list. — The names. The concerns. The praise points. The ongoing requests. The list keeps her from forgetting. The list keeps her praying for people she genuinely loves. The list becomes, over years, a record of answered prayer she did not notice happening.

She prays specifically — not generally. — "Bless everyone" is not a prayer. "Heal Susan's knee, restore her mobility, give her patience through the physical therapy" is a prayer. She names the specific thing. She lets specificity be her teacher.

She prays scripture back to God. — She takes the Psalms and makes them her own. She takes the promises and holds God to them. She prays the petitions of the early church for her own household. The woman who has learned to pray scripture has learned to pray in God's own language.

She prays for her enemies. — The person who hurt her. The coworker who undermined her. The family member who betrayed her. Not because the enemy deserves it. Because Jesus said to. And she has found, over years, that praying for an enemy is one of the only ways to be freed from hating them.

She prays before she speaks. — Before the hard conversation. Before the important email. Before the confrontation. A whispered prayer in the thirty seconds before she acts. It does not take time. It changes what follows.

She prays over the house. — Room by room, occasionally. Over her children's beds. Over the dinner table. Over the threshold. The home is spiritual territory. She claims it in prayer. She does not abandon it to whatever drifts in.

She prays boldly — as a daughter, not a beggar. — She has read the invitation. "Let us then with confidence draw near to the throne of grace." She comes boldly. She asks for much. She does not pray like a stranger at the gate. She prays like a child at the table.

She listens. — Prayer is not only speaking. Sometimes it is silence, waiting, hearing. The woman who has learned to listen in prayer hears things the hurried pray-er never hears. She leaves space for the Lord to speak.

She prays in secret. — Most of her prayers no one else will ever hear. This is not a deficit. This is what Jesus said to do. The Father who sees in secret rewards her. The woman whose prayer life is public is often the woman whose prayer life is shallow. Depth happens where no one is looking.

List 5: Ten Ways to Stand When Everything Around You Is Falling

Stand on what is unshakeable. — The Lord does not change. His word does not change. His love for his people does not change. When the world is shaking, she puts her feet on what cannot be moved. She does not stand on feelings. She does not stand on circumstances. She stands on him.

Do not panic. — Panic is the enemy's tool. He uses it to push her into decisions she will regret. The woman who has learned to breathe, to wait, to not react in the moment — is a woman who does not get stampeded. She pauses. She breathes. She prays. Then she acts.

Do not rewrite your theology in the middle of a crisis. — The crisis will tempt her to throw out what she believed in better times. Do not. The theology that was sound in the sunshine is still sound in the storm. She does not abandon it because it is hard. The hard is exactly when it is tested.

Hold onto the hand of someone wiser. — Her pastor. Her mentor. Her mother. An older believer. The woman in the middle of a storm needs a hand to hold. Someone who has been through something similar. Someone who can say, "I have been here. You will get through."

Keep doing the next right thing. — Not the thing ten steps from now. The next thing. The morning prayer. The breakfast for the kids. The email that has to be sent. The faithful small act, compounded, becomes a life in a storm. She does what is in front of her, and then the next thing, and then the next.

Do not isolate yourself. — The storm pulls her toward isolation. Fight it. Be with people. Go to church. Go to the small group. Keep the friendships alive. The woman who isolates in a crisis is the woman who gets buried. Stay connected.

Preach the gospel to yourself daily. — She reminds herself who she is. Loved. Forgiven. Sealed. Adopted. Held. The gospel is not just the doorway into faith. It is the floor she stands on every day of the life that follows. She rehearses it. She believes it. She stands on it.

Fast, sometimes. — The discipline of going without — a meal, the phone, a comfort — sharpens the soul. The Lord himself pointed to fasting as a spiritual weapon. She does not use it performatively. She uses it when her soul needs sharper edges. It works.

Worship — even when you do not feel like it. — Sing. Or play the song and let it sing for you. Worship bends the soul back toward truth. The woman who worships in the middle of a storm is a woman whose soul is being straightened under the weight. She does not wait to feel like worshiping. She worships until the feeling returns.

Know that he is standing with you. — You are not holding yourself up. He is holding you. The woman who stands in a crisis is standing because someone larger than her is standing behind her. This is not self-reliance. This is supernatural reliance. She is held. She will stand.

List 6: Ten Pieces of the Spiritual Arsenal a Woman Cannot Do Without

The Word. — Not as a decoration. As a weapon. The verses she has memorized are the sword she can actually swing. She cannot pull it out if she has not put it in. She carries the Word in her head and her heart because there are fights she will face where her phone is not available.

Prayer — as daily breath, not occasional crisis call. — The woman who prays only in emergencies will find her line crackles in the emergency. The woman who has been praying for decades will find the line is clear. Keep the line open.

The name of Jesus. — She speaks it. In the moment of temptation. In the moment of fear. In the moment of attack. "Jesus." It is not a magic word. It is the name above every name, and it has authority she can invoke. She does not hesitate to use it.

The sacraments. — The bread and the cup, taken regularly. The reminder, physical and visible, of what he has done. The woman who partakes regularly is a woman who is being fed by the One she is following. Do not skip it when you can take it.

The community of believers. — The local church. The small group. The one friend who will call you to account. You cannot fight spiritual battles alone. You were not designed to. The arsenal includes other people.

Worship music — for the commute, the kitchen, the walk. — Songs saturated with truth. The worship playlist is not entertainment. It is equipment. The songs go in through the ears and stay with you long after the speaker is off. Choose what is playing in your head. Feed yourself truth.

Solitude with God — regularly. — The quiet morning. The walk alone. The day in nature. The woman who never has time alone with God becomes a woman running on the fumes of borrowed faith. She builds in the solitude. She cannot skip it without paying.

Godly counsel — accessed before the crisis. — Her pastor. Her mentor. Her friend who knows the scripture and loves her. She builds the relationships in peacetime so she has them in wartime. Do not wait until the attack to find your counselors.

Confession — to God, to a person. — The sin confessed loses much of its power. The sin kept in the dark grows. The woman who has one person she confesses to — a trusted friend, a spouse, a pastor — has a weapon against secrecy. Darkness is the enemy's habitat. She lets in light.

The armor of God — worn daily. — The belt of truth. The breastplate of righteousness. The shoes of the gospel of peace. The shield of faith. The helmet of salvation. The sword of the Spirit. Not metaphors only. Postures. Practices. She puts them on — consciously, some mornings literally — before she goes out.

List 7: Ten Ways to See God in the Ordinary

In the light through the kitchen window at 7 a.m. — The morning light is not secular. It is, every morning, an act of creation. The woman who notices the light is noticing a daily gift the Lord is extending to her. She gives thanks for the light. She lets the ordinary become an altar.

In the children's faces at the breakfast table. — They are made in his image. The woman who looks at her children and sees his fingerprints is living inside a miracle she has stopped seeing because it became routine. Look again. Thank him again.

In the meal she did not think she could afford. — The provision came. The way opened. The bill was paid. She notices. She says thank you. She tells her children. The ordinary provisions are not accidents of commerce. They are a Father feeding his daughter.

In the conversation that turned at the exact right moment. — The friend who called when she was at her lowest. The text that came exactly when she needed it. The door that opened when she was ready to give up. These are not coincidences. She recognizes them. She says thank you.

In the answered prayer she forgot she prayed. — The petition from two years ago, granted last week. She would not have recognized it as an answer if she had not remembered praying it. She keeps the list so she can notice. Noticing is half of gratitude.

In the scripture verse that reappeared at the exact right season. — The verse she read at twenty-five that now, at forty, means what she did not know it could mean. The Word is alive. It speaks to different seasons in different voices. She is ready to hear when it does.

In the hymn that rose up in her at the hard moment. — The hymn her grandmother sang. The song she had not thought of in years. It returned — at the exact hour she needed it. The Spirit preserves what the soul has stored up. She keeps storing.

Do not let the battle become your identity. — The woman who is always in a spiritual fight and talks about nothing else has made the fight her god. She fights what needs fighting. She does not define herself by the fighting. Her identity is in Christ, not in the battles.

Pick your battles — with discernment. — Not every disagreement is a hill. Not every provocation is a call to war. The woman who engages every fight is a woman who has lost her sense of proportion. She asks: Is this worth my peace? Often the answer is no. She lets it go.

Do not personalize every attack. — The attack came from the enemy, not primarily from the person. The husband was not her enemy. The coworker was not her enemy. The child in rebellion was not her enemy. The fight is in the unseen realm. She aims her prayer accordingly. She does not aim her rage at the person.

Be quick to forgive — even in the middle of the battle. — Bitterness is a slow poison. The woman who does not forgive is carrying the enemy's work inside her soul. She forgives. Not because the person has earned it. Because her own peace requires it.

Rest. Eat. Sleep. — Spiritual warfare is physically taxing. The woman who is not caring for her body in the middle of the battle is a woman who will soon be unable to fight. She takes the walks. She eats the meals. She sleeps the nights. The battle is not a license to neglect the basics. It is a reason to maintain them.

Laugh. — The enemy hates the laughter of a confident daughter of God. Laugh often. At yourself. At the absurdity of the enemy's lies. At the joy still present in the middle of hard days. Laughter is a weapon. Use it.

Keep your marriage alive in the middle of the warfare. — Do not let the battle consume the partnership. Date your husband. Talk to him. Laugh with him. Build together. The marriage is its own frontline, and the enemy wants to use every other battle to erode it. She defends the marriage first.

Celebrate the small victories. — The prayer answered. The door opened. The child who had a good day. The temptation resisted. The enemy wants her to only see what is still broken. She notices what is being healed. She gives thanks out loud. The thanksgiving itself is a weapon.

Hand the whole thing back to God — at the end of every day. — Before you sleep, lay it down. The children, the marriage, the work, the fear, the fight. Put them in his hands. You are not the rescuer of your own life. He is. She releases. She sleeps. He does not sleep, and he does not stop working. She trusts that.

List 10: Ten Things a Woman Who Finishes Faithful Has Known

Jesus is enough. — The rest was addition. The husband, if she had one. The children, if she had them. The work, the friendships, the health, the years. All of these were gifts — but none of them, finally, was the point. The point was him. The woman who has finished faithful has known this for a long time.

The Bible was true. — Every promise she staked her life on held. The Lord did what he said he would do. She was not naive to trust it. She was wise. The word she leaned on did not fail. It will not fail you either. Hold it.

Suffering was not the final word. — She suffered. More than some. She did not choose it. But she did not waste it. She let it form her. She let it deepen her. She finished her suffering, and her suffering finished its work in her, and she emerged with a depth the unsuffering do not have.

The small faithfulness mattered more than she knew at the time. — The prayers she prayed when no one was watching. The children she raised one day at a time. The work she did faithfully year after year. The meals she made. The conversations she had. It all mattered. She just could not see it until she could look back.

The people she loved were the treasure. — Not the things. Not the accomplishments. The people. Her husband. Her children. Her friends. Her church. Her neighbors. The relationships she tended became the only wealth she brought with her to the end. She was right to invest there.

Forgiveness was worth it — every time. — The grudge she did not hold. The offense she did not nurse. The resentment she did not carry. Forgiveness had cost her something, but bitterness would have cost more. She chose rightly. Her soul, at the end, is lighter than the soul of the woman who never forgave.

The Lord was faithful in every season. — The early seasons when she first met him. The middle seasons when she was figuring it out. The hard seasons when she wondered if he was there. The long seasons of waiting. The late seasons of fruit-bearing. He was there, in every one. She sees it now.

Eternity is not a metaphor. — It is a real place. He is really there. The loved ones who went before her are really there. The reunion is real. The home is real. She knows this not because she is a wishful thinker. She knows this because he promised it, and everything else he promised has come true.

Death is a doorway, not a wall. — She had been taught to fear it. The Lord has been teaching her, quietly, for years, that it is a passage. She has stopped fearing. She has, in the late years, sometimes anticipated. The woman who has walked with him is not afraid of the last step. She has been holding his hand for a long time.

The crown is laid up for her. — The Lord has prepared it. It was not earned. It was prepared. She will not strut in with it. She will lay it down at his feet — because every crown is his, really, and the laying down is the worship she has been practicing her whole life. She has finished faithful. The crown is there. He is there. It is all there. It is worth everything it cost.

FAITH & SPIRITUAL WARFARE: QUOTES WORTH REMEMBERING

"For our struggle is not against flesh and blood, but against the spiritual forces of evil." — Adapted from Ephesians 6:12

"Put on the full armor of God, so that you can take your stand against the devil's schemes." — Ephesians 6:11

"Fervent prayer keeps your true identity in focus." — Priscilla Shirer, Fervent

"Greater is he who is in you than he who is in the world." — 1 John 4:4

"All of reality is engraced." — Abigail Favale, Into the Deep

"Resist the devil, and he will flee from you." — James 4:7

"Repentance requires greater intimacy with God than with our sin." — Attributed to Rosaria Butterfield

"Submit yourselves, then, to God. Draw near to God and He will draw near to you." — Adapted from James 4:7-8

"I don't shy away from singing about my faith." — Lauren Daigle, Billboard interview

"You have no idea the fire that you have ignited within this wife." — Erika Kirk, Phoenix memorial, 2025

FAITH & SPIRITUAL WARFARE: PUTTING IT INTO PRACTICE

Start the day with ten minutes of the Word — for thirty days. — Not on the phone. The actual book. Begin with a gospel. Read. Underline. Pray a sentence back. Ten minutes. Thirty days. See what shifts in you.

Memorize one passage of scripture this month — to have when you need it. — Psalm 23. Psalm 91. Isaiah 41:10. Ephesians 6:10--18. Choose one. Write it out. Repeat it until it lives inside you. You are building an arsenal for the day you will need it.

Identify the lie you hear most often — and write the truth that counters it — Write both on a card. Keep the card where you will see it. When the lie comes, read the truth out loud. Do it every time the lie returns. Retrain the voice in your head.

Pray for your children — specifically — every day this week. — Name each child. Name one specific thing for each. Do it out loud. Do it often. Your prayer is the weapon no school program and no YouTube video can substitute for.

Fast from one thing for one week. — The phone. A meal. A show. A habit. Let the removal create space. Use the space to pray. The fast is not about the thing. It is about the re-centering on the Lord.

Confess one thing to one trusted person this week. — Not to the world. Not on the internet. To one person who loves you and will pray for you. The sin carried in darkness grows. The sin confessed begins to lose its grip.

Put on the armor of God — deliberately — in the morning. — Read Ephesians 6. Pray it on, piece by piece. Do it for one week as an experiment. See how you walk differently into the day.

Refuse the enemy's voice out loud — in the name of Jesus. — "In the name of Jesus, I reject this lie." "In the name of Jesus, I claim the truth of who I am." "In the name of Jesus, I command this fear to go." He flees. James 4:7 is not a metaphor. Speak it.

Tell one other woman what the Lord has done for you — this month. — Not on social media. In person or on the phone. A testimony is a weapon. Sharing it strengthens you and her. Break the silence. Say what he has done.

Write your own creed — what you will stand on when everything else falls. — One page. In your own words. What you believe about God. What you believe about Jesus. What you believe about yourself. What you will not let go of, no matter what comes. Sign it. Keep it. Read it on the hard days. You are a daughter of the King. Stand like it.

CONCLUSION

A WORD FOR THE WOMAN WHO MADE IT TO THE END

If you are reading this page, you have walked with me through one hundred lists. You have read ten chapters. You have met a version of womanhood that the culture does not often put into words — fierce and tender, submitted and strong, traditional in the deepest sense and unafraid of any of it.

I did not write this book to tell you who you should be.

I wrote it to remind you of who you already are — and to hand you some of the standards that the women who came before you carried quietly, without being able to articulate, because the culture had not yet tried to erase them.

It has tried now. Much of what a woman once inherited as common sense is now treated as contested territory. The idea that her body is not public property. The idea that motherhood is not a career setback. The idea that a husband is a partner and not a threat. The idea that modesty is self-respect rather than self-hatred. The idea that she is not in a competition with her friends. The idea that her worth was fixed before the world ever had an opinion about her face.

These were once the water she swam in.

Now she has to choose them, defend them, and pass them down on purpose.

That is your task. It has been the task of every generation of faithful women since Eve. You are not doing something strange. You are doing what your grandmother's grandmother did — just in harder conditions, with fewer allies, in louder rooms.

You can do it.

I wrote the companion to this book, *The Forgotten Standards for Men,* because I believe men have forgotten what it is to be men — and because the recovery of masculinity is essential to the recovery of the common life. I wrote this book because I believe women have been handed a lie even more comprehensive than the one handed to men, and the recovery of womanhood is just as essential. Neither recovery can happen without the other. Men and women were made to walk beside each other. When one side collapses, the other does too.

I am a man writing for women. I know that is unusual. I have written carefully. I have written everything I have written here with my wife beside me and my daughter in mind and the God who made us both watching. I have not tried to flatter you. I have not tried to offend you. I have tried to tell the truth — with reverence for what you have been given and with honesty about what you are up against.

If any of these one hundred lists has reminded you of a thing you already knew but had stopped saying, I have done the work I set out to do.

If any of them has made you uncomfortable — sit with the discomfort. Ask what in you is resisting. Some of the resistance is the Holy Spirit pulling you back to what you were made for. Some of it is the culture you have absorbed more deeply than you realized. You will know the difference. Pray about it. Bring it to the Lord. Let him do the sorting.

Do not try to live all one hundred lists at once. That is not how formation works. Take one. Live with it for a season. Return to this book in a year and take another. The Christian life is a long obedience in the same direction, and the standards in this book are not a checklist to be completed in a month. They are a landscape you will be walking for the rest of your life.

I want you to know something that the world will not tell you.

You are not too late.

Whatever season you are in, whatever you have done, whatever has been done to you, whatever ground you thought you had lost — you are not too late. The Lord has redeemed women older than you, more broken than you, more far from him than you. He has done it every generation. He is doing it in yours. He is not going to stop when it comes to you.

The Samaritan woman who had been with five husbands was entrusted with the first city-wide gospel proclamation in the Gospel of John. The woman who had been bleeding for twelve years reached for the hem of his garment and was healed. The woman who anointed his feet with ointment in the house of Simon was commended when every man in the room criticized her. The women at the tomb, who had come to anoint a dead body, were given the first word of the resurrection — before the apostles knew, before Peter knew, before the world knew.

This is the Lord you are dealing with.

He has never looked at women the way the world looks at women. He has looked at you with tenderness since before you had a face. He looks at you now with no condemnation. He will look at you on the last day with the welcome of a Father who has been waiting for you the whole time.

Finish faithful.

That is what I want for you. That is what your mothers wanted for you. That is what the Lord is calling you to. Finish faithful — through the young years and the middle years and the long years. Through the marriages and the motherhoods and the work. Through the sorrows that will come and the joys that will surprise you. Through the seasons when you feel fierce and the seasons when you feel fragile. Finish faithful.

At the end of the race, there is a crown. You will not strut in with it. You will lay it at his feet. Every crown is his. That is the worship you have been practicing your whole life — the laying down of what you thought was yours at the feet of the One who was yours all along.

Go be the woman he made you to be.

The standards are not forgotten if one woman remembers them.

You remember them now. Live them. Pass them down.

God be with you.

—*Geoffrey Arbuckle*

Kansas City, Missouri

APPENDIX A

This is a partial index of the scripture quoted, paraphrased, or alluded to across the ten categories. It is not comprehensive. It is provided for the reader who wants to return to a passage, study the context, or use this book as a devotional alongside her Bible.

The Lord's own word always outweighs any book written about it. If a single verse in this list leads you back into your Bible more often, this appendix has done its job.

GENESIS

- 1:27 — Male and female he created them.

- 2:18 — It is not good for man to be alone.

- 2:24 — A man shall leave his father and mother and hold fast to his wife.

EXODUS

- 20:8--11 — Remember the Sabbath day, to keep it holy.

- 20:12 — Honor your father and your mother.

RUTH

- 1:16 — Where you go, I will go; where you lodge, I will lodge. Your people shall be my people, and your God my God.

1 SAMUEL

- 1:10--20 — Hannah's prayer for a son.

- 16:7 — The Lord looks on the heart.

PSALMS

- 1 — Blessed is the man who walks not in the counsel of the wicked.

- 23 — The Lord is my shepherd.

- 27:14 — Wait for the Lord; be strong, and let your heart take courage.

- 30:5 — Weeping may tarry for the night, but joy comes with the morning.

- 46:10 — Be still, and know that I am God.

- 91 — He who dwells in the shelter of the Most High.

- 127:3 — Children are a heritage from the Lord.

- 139:13--14 — You formed my inward parts; you knitted me together in my mother's womb.

- 145:4 — One generation shall commend your works to another.

PROVERBS

- 3:5--6 — Trust in the Lord with all your heart, and do not lean on your own understanding.

- 17:17 — A friend loves at all times.

- 22:1 — A good name is to be chosen rather than great riches.

- 22:6 — Train up a child in the way he should go.

- 27:17 — Iron sharpens iron.

- 31:10--31 — The Wife of Noble Character (the complete portrait of Proverbs 31).

ECCLESIASTES

- 3:1 — For everything there is a season.

- 4:9--10 — Two are better than one.

SONG OF SONGS

- 8:6--7 — Set me as a seal upon your heart. Love is strong as death.

ISAIAH

- 26:3 — You keep him in perfect peace whose mind is stayed on you.

- 40:30--31 — Those who hope in the Lord will renew their strength.

- 41:10 — Fear not, for I am with you.

- 54:17 — No weapon formed against you shall prosper.

- 55:8--9 — My thoughts are not your thoughts.

JEREMIAH

- 29:11 — I know the plans I have for you.

- 31:3 — I have loved you with an everlasting love.

LAMENTATIONS

- 3:22--23 — The steadfast love of the Lord never ceases; his mercies are new every morning.

MATTHEW

- 5:14--16 — You are the light of the world. Let your light shine.

- 6:6 — Go into your room, shut the door, and pray to your Father who is in secret.

- 6:19--21 — Do not lay up for yourselves treasures on earth.

- 6:25--34 — Do not be anxious about your life.

- 11:28--30 — Come to me, all who labor and are heavy laden.

- 22:37--39 — You shall love the Lord your God... and your neighbor as yourself.

MARK

- 5:25--34 — The woman who reached for the hem of Jesus' garment.

- 12:41--44 — The widow's two mites.

LUKE

- 1:38 — Let it be to me according to your word. (Mary's yes.)

- 1:46--55 — The Magnificat.

- 10:38--42 — Martha and Mary.

- 15:11--32 — The prodigal son and the waiting Father.

- 23:55--24:11 — The women at the cross and the empty tomb.

JOHN

- 4:1--42 — The Samaritan woman at the well.

- 8:1--11 — The woman caught in adultery.

- 11:25--26 — I am the resurrection and the life.

- 14:27 — Peace I leave with you; my peace I give to you.

- 15:12--13 — Greater love has no one than this, that someone lay down his life for his friends.

- 20:11--18 — Mary Magdalene at the empty tomb.

ACTS

- 9:36--42 — Dorcas (Tabitha), a disciple full of good works.

- 16:13--15 — Lydia, a worshiper of God.

ROMANS

- 5:3--5 — Suffering produces endurance, and endurance character.

- 8:28 — All things work together for good for those who love God.

- 12:2 — Be transformed by the renewal of your mind.

- 12:12 — Rejoice in hope, be patient in tribulation, be constant in prayer.

1 CORINTHIANS

- 6:19--20 — Your body is a temple of the Holy Spirit.

- 10:13 — No temptation has overtaken you that is not common to man.

- 10:31 — Whether you eat or drink, do all to the glory of God.

- 13 — The love chapter.

2 CORINTHIANS

- 10:5 — Take every thought captive to obey Christ.

- 12:9 — My grace is sufficient for you, for my power is made perfect in weakness.

GALATIANS

- 5:22–23 — The fruit of the Spirit.

- 6:9 — Let us not grow weary of doing good.

EPHESIANS

- 2:8–9 — By grace you have been saved through faith.

- 4:2 — With all humility and gentleness, with patience, bearing with one another in love.

- 4:32 — Be kind to one another, tenderhearted, forgiving one another.

- 5:25–33 — Husbands, love your wives.

- 6:10–18 — The armor of God.

PHILIPPIANS

- 1:6 — He who began a good work in you will bring it to completion.

- 4:4–8 — Rejoice in the Lord always. Do not be anxious about anything.

- 4:13 — I can do all things through him who strengthens me.

COLOSSIANS

- 3:12 — Put on compassionate hearts, kindness, humility, meekness, and patience.

- 3:23 — Whatever you do, work heartily, as for the Lord.

1 THESSALONIANS

- 5:16–18 — Rejoice always, pray without ceasing, give thanks in all circumstances.

1 TIMOTHY

- 4:8 — Bodily training is of some value, but godliness is of value in every way.

2 TIMOTHY

- 1:5 — Timothy's faith, inherited from his grandmother Lois and his mother Eunice.

- 1:7 — God has not given us a spirit of fear, but of power and of love and of a sound mind.

- 4:7--8 — I have fought the good fight, I have finished the race, I have kept the faith.

HEBREWS

- 4:16 — Let us then with confidence draw near to the throne of grace.

- 10:24--25 — Let us consider how to stir up one another to love and good works.

- 11 — The Hall of Faith.

- 12:1--2 — Surrounded by so great a cloud of witnesses.

- 13:5 — He has said, "I will never leave you nor forsake you."

- 13:16 — Do not neglect to do good and to share what you have.

JAMES

- 1:2--4 — Count it all joy when you meet trials of various kinds.

- 1:19 — Let every person be quick to hear, slow to speak, slow to anger.

- 4:7 — Submit yourselves therefore to God. Resist the devil, and he will flee from you.

1 PETER

- 3:3--4 — Let your adorning be the hidden person of the heart, with the imperishable beauty of a gentle and quiet spirit.

- 5:7 — Cast all your anxieties on him, because he cares for you.

1 JOHN

- 1:9 — If we confess our sins, he is faithful and just to forgive us.

- 3:18 — Little children, let us not love in word or talk but in deed and in truth.

- 4:4 — Greater is he that is in you, than he that is in the world.

- 4:18 — Perfect love casts out fear.

- 4:19 — We love because he first loved us.

REVELATION

- 12:11 — They have conquered him by the blood of the Lamb and by the word of their testimony.

- 21:4 — He will wipe away every tear.

APPENDIX B

These are books I have found useful, alongside scripture, in the formation of women and of families. I do not agree with every sentence of every author listed. No reader should. The point of a reading list is not uniformity of opinion. The point is exposure to voices worth reckoning with.

Read widely. Read across traditions. Read old books more than new ones. Let the dead authors have as much time on your shelf as the living ones.

THE BIBLE

Read it first. Read it last. Read it between. No list of recommended reading belongs on the same page as scripture, except to point back to it. If you read only one book for the rest of your life, read this one — again and again. It reads you back.

ON WOMANHOOD AND IDENTITY

Elisabeth Elliot — *Let Me Be a Woman*, *Passion and Purity*, *These Strange Ashes*, *The Shaping of a Christian Family*. Elliot wrote from the soil of her own suffering and her own marriage, and her voice is one of the clearest of the twentieth century.

Edith Schaeffer — *The Hidden Art of Homemaking*, *What Is a Family?* Schaeffer saw the home as a place of cultural creation and meaningful beauty. Her writing rescues the ordinary domestic work from the sentimental and the dismissive alike.

Rebekah Merkle — *Eve in Exile*. A book that takes seriously both the secular account of women and the biblical one, and finds the secular account wanting.

Nancy Wilson — *The Fruit of Her Hands*, *Building Her House*. A practical theology of wife and mother.

Alisa Childers — *Another Gospel?*, *Live Your Truth and Other Lies*. A former Christian worship artist whose encounter with progressive Christianity drove her back to the historic faith, and whose writing models how to think about both.

ON MARRIAGE

Kathy Keller — *The Meaning of Marriage* (contributions and chapter). Keller brings the practical wisdom of a long marriage alongside a theologically careful treatment of the covenant itself.

Francine Rivers — *Redeeming Love*. A novel that retells the book of Hosea in the American West. Transformative for many women.

Erika Kirk — public remarks and Phoenix memorial address, 2025. A young widow's public testimony to the costliness and the gift of Christian marriage, delivered in front of a nation that did not expect it.

ON MOTHERHOOD

Sally Clarkson — *The Mission of Motherhood*, *Own Your Life*, *The Life-giving Home* (with Sarah Clarkson). Clarkson has given a generation of mothers a vocabulary for treating the home as a cultivated place and motherhood as a calling worth the whole self.

Rachel Jankovic — *Loving the Little Years*, *Fit to Burst*. Short, sharp, honest essays from a mother who refuses to romanticize or catastrophize the work.

Gloria Furman — *Missional Motherhood*, *Treasuring Christ When Your Hands Are Full*. Theologically grounded and gently practical.

Ainsley Earhardt — *The Light Within Me*. A working mother's memoir about faith, family, and the costs and rewards of a public career.

ON PRAYER AND THE INNER LIFE

Priscilla Shirer — *Fervent*, *The Resolution for Women*. A book on prayer and spiritual warfare for women, from a teacher whose voice is distinctively her own.

Ruth Bell Graham — *Sitting by My Laughing Fire, Legacy of a Pack Rat.* A poet writing about the real work of loving God in the middle of the real work of loving people.

Jennie Allen — *Get Out of Your Head, Find Your People, Restless.* Allen teaches the practical work of disciplining the mind and building honest community.

Nancy DeMoss Wolgemuth — *Choosing Gratitude, Lies Women Believe and the Truth that Sets Them Free.* Wolgemuth is a careful, patient teacher whose long ministry on Revive Our Hearts has discipled a generation of women.

ON SUFFERING AND SPIRITUAL FORMATION

Joni Eareckson Tada — *A Place of Healing, Making Sense of Suffering.* Tada has lived with quadriplegia for more than five decades and has written from inside suffering with unusual honesty and unusual trust.

Corrie ten Boom — *The Hiding Place.* A Dutch Christian family sheltered Jews during the Nazi occupation of the Netherlands. What followed is one of the most honest accounts of forgiveness in modern memory.

Elisabeth Elliot — *Through Gates of Splendor, Shadow of the Almighty.* The story of her first husband's martyrdom and her subsequent return to the people who killed him.

Hannah Whitall Smith — *The Christian's Secret of a Happy Life.* An older book, written in an older idiom, still useful.

Lysa TerKeurst — *It's Not Supposed to Be This Way, Unglued, Uninvited.* TerKeurst writes out of her own hardest seasons — a cancer diagnosis, a near-divorce, a long rebuilding — and her readers keep returning because the work is honest.

ON THEOLOGY AND DOCTRINE FOR WOMEN WHO WANT MORE

Jen Wilkin — *Women of the Word, None Like Him, In His Image.* Wilkin teaches women to study the Bible as a thinking discipline rather than only a devotional one.

Nancy Guthrie — *Even Better Than Eden, The One Year Book of Hope, Seeing Jesus in the Old Testament* (series). Guthrie models what it looks like to read the whole Bible as one story about one Savior.

Kelly Needham — *Friend-ish: Reclaiming Real Friendship in a Culture of Confusion.* A book for women who have taken their relationships seriously and then found them complicated.

Jackie Hill Perry — *Gay Girl, Good God, Holier Than Thou.* Hill Perry brings a poet's ear and a convert's clarity to questions of identity, sexuality, and the holiness of God.

ON CULTURAL DISCERNMENT

Mary Harrington — *Feminism Against Progress.* A secular British writer who has concluded that the progressive feminism of her own generation has cost women more than it has delivered. Not a Christian book. Worth reading.

Abigail Favale — *The Genesis of Gender, Into the Deep.* A former postmodern feminist who came into the Catholic Church and wrote an honest accounting of what she saw in both places.

Mary Eberstadt — *Home-Alone America, Primal Screams.* Eberstadt is one of the few public intellectuals who has taken the destruction of the family seriously enough to chart its downstream effects.

Rosaria Butterfield — *The Secret Thoughts of an Unlikely Convert, Openness Unhindered, The Gospel Comes with a House Key.* A former lesbian English professor whose conversion, writing, and hospitality have reframed how many women think about both repentance and home.

Allie Beth Stuckey — *You're Not Enough (and That's Ok), Toxic Empathy.* Stuckey takes apart the slogans of the self-love culture with a directness that has made her both beloved and controversial.

OLDER VOICES (READ THEM)

Amy Carmichael — *If, A Chance to Die.* An Irish missionary who spent fifty-five years in India rescuing girls from temple prostitution. Her devotional writing is severe and useful.

Teresa of Ávila — *The Interior Castle*. A sixteenth-century Spanish nun whose account of the soul's movement toward God has spoken across every denominational boundary.

Julian of Norwich — *Revelations of Divine Love*. Medieval England. Short. Luminous.

Hildegard of Bingen — *Scivias, The Book of Divine Works*. A twelfth-century German abbess whose visions, music, and writing outlasted most of her more famous male contemporaries.

Catherine of Siena — *The Dialogue*. A fourteenth-century Italian mystic whose correspondence and counsel reached popes and princes and whose honesty is still bracing.

FOR YOUR CHILDREN

Sally Lloyd-Jones — *The Jesus Storybook Bible*. The single best children's bible written in English.

Sarah Mackenzie — *Read-Aloud Revival* (the podcast and website, alongside her books). A gift for the mother who wants to raise children who actually read.

Karen Swallow Prior — *On Reading Well, The Evangelical Imagination*. For the mother who is raising the next generation and wants to think carefully about what she is putting in her children's hands.

A FINAL NOTE

No one has time to read all of these. Pick one. Read it slowly. Live with it for a while. Let it do its work.

The woman who reads twelve real books in a year is a woman being formed. The woman who reads a hundred articles a week on the feed is being formed too — but into someone else. Choose what is forming you.

Read the old more than the new. Read the hard more than the easy. Read across the tradition, not only within your own corner of it. Come back to the Bible more than you go anywhere else.

The inner life of a woman is built, in part, out of what she reads. Build well.

APPENDIX C

INDEX OF THE 100 LISTS

This is the full map of the book — every list, in order, under the category to which it belongs. Use it to find what you need when you need it.

CATEGORY 1 — WOMANHOOD & IDENTITY

CATEGORY 2 — SISTERHOOD

CATEGORY 3 — MOTHERHOOD

List 1: Ten Things Every Mother Needs to Know Before She Starts

List 2: Ten Lies the Culture Tells Mothers

List 3: Ten Ways to Raise a Daughter Who Knows Her Worth

List 4: Ten Ways to Raise a Son Who Respects Women

List 5: Ten Things to Say to Your Children Every Week

List 6: Ten Things Never to Say to Your Children

List 7: Ten Ways to Discipline Without Crushing Their Spirit

List 8: Ten Ways to Pass Down a Living Faith

List 9: Ten Ways to Mother When You're Running on Empty

List 10: Ten Ways to Release Them Well

CATEGORY 4 — MARRIAGE & DEVOTION

List 1: Ten Marks of a Marriage Built to Last

List 2: Ten Lies the Culture Tells Wives

List 3: Ten Things Every Wife Should Know About Her
Husband

List 4: Ten Ways to Respect Him Without Losing Yourself

List 5: Ten Ways to Be a Safe Place for Him to Come
Home To

List 6: Ten Conversations to Have Before the Wedding

List 7: Ten Fights Worth Having — and Ten Not To

List 8: Ten Ways to Protect Your Marriage From the
Outside World

List 9: Ten Ways to Love Him When You Don't Feel Like
It

List 10: Ten Ways to Rebuild When the Marriage Is
Breaking

CATEGORY 5 — LEADERSHIP

List 1: Ten Marks of a Woman Who Leads Without Apology

List 2: Ten Things That Happen When a Woman Leads Among Men

List 3: Ten Ways to Command Respect Without Demanding It

List 4: Ten Ways Women Lead Differently — and Why That's a Gift

List 5: Ten Ways to Mentor the Next Generation of Women

List 6: Ten Ways to Take a Stand Without Burning the Bridge

List 7: Ten Ways to Lead at Home

List 8: Ten Ways to Lead in Church

List 9: Ten Ways to Lead When No One Is Watching

List 10: Ten Truths About What a Woman's Leadership Leaves Behind

List 1: Ten Ways to Know What You Were Made to Do

List 2: Ten Lies the World Tells Women About Work

List 3: Ten Ways to Carry Your Faith into Your Work

List 4: Ten Things to Remember When the Workplace
Wasn't Built for You

List 5: Ten Signs It's Time to Stay — or Go

List 6: Ten Ways to Pursue Excellence Without Making It
an Idol

List 7: Ten Ways to Handle Money Wisely as a Woman

List 8: Ten Ways to Find Purpose in Ordinary Work

List 9: Ten Ways to Balance Ambition and Surrender

List 10: Ten Ways to Finish Your Working Years Well

CATEGORY 7 — PHYSICAL DISCIPLINE

CATEGORY 8 — MENTAL & EMOTIONAL STRENGTH

❧

List 1: Ten Things a Woman Leaves Behind — and What She Does Not

List 2: Ten Ways to Influence Without a Platform

List 3: Ten Ways to Make the Room Better for the Women Who Come After You

List 4: Ten Ways to Mentor Without an Agenda

List 5: Ten Ways to Speak Life Into the People Around You

List 6: Ten Things to Pass Down on Purpose

List 7: Ten Ways to Let Your Children Watch You Live — and Benefit From the Watching

List 8: Ten Marks of a Woman Who Will Be Remembered Well

List 9: Ten Things to Build That Will Outlive You

List 10: Ten Ways to Finish Your Life With More Than You Started With

❦

❦

One hundred lists. Ten thousand words of truth, distilled. A map for the whole of a woman's life — not because she will master all of it, but because she will need all of it at some point along the way.

Return to it as often as you need.